To: Sebrina
7/1/2020

I Don't Want to Be That

by

Timothy Keys

Thank you for the support!
Hope and pray you enjoy the read.

[signature]

First Edition: October 2018

Lenox Avenue Publishing

www. lenoxavenuepublishing.virb.com

Printed in the United States of America

Table of Contents

Chapter 1: "This Is Me"

Song by: Keala Settle and The Greatest Showman 2017

People who know me now have said some flattering things about me. I've heard affirming comments like "Why he so happy"; "That boy ain't never change"; "You are always so positive"; "Oh you don't know Timothy Keys?"; "Mayor of midtown"; "Hairstylist to the stars"; "He's the life of the party"; "Your laugh is infectious!". Hearing these words spoken not only boosts my self-confidence but empower me in my work as well. I am that guy you can catch a glimpse of doing hair or makeup through the huge windows of a very cute boutique style hair salon located in the heart of midtown Atlanta; all while I was making the world a more beautiful place one person at a time. I have been a hairstylist for seven years as of 2018 and love what I do, who I do it with and for. After hours, if you dare, one may catch me walking the streets of midtown, spot me at my favorite watering hole, bar hopping, or off to a movie, musical, play or concert. I am a lover of the arts and local theater productions. Those who encounter me affirm that I am known for my positive attitude. I am the type of guy that is always smiling, happy, upbeat and friendly. I am always ready to give a compliment at any given moment to strangers in passing. Yep that is me, I am that guy. I am also that guy that hates being called out of his name.

My birth certificate has Timothy Keys printed on it, my parents named me that and it is what I prefer to be called. The name Timothy means to honor God or honored by God. Now, my best friend calls me "Chipmunk" and has for over the past fifteen years or so because of my slightly chubby cheeks. HE IS THE ONLY ONE!!! To everyone else I am Timothy, Timothy Keys. I respond a few different ways when it comes to someone who calls me anything but my name. Below are the three reactions to those people:

- Ignore – To the people that I feel I will not or do not want to change; or someone I don't know well or hell in that case don't want to get to know. I will simply ignore them or slightly turn my head away from them as a gesture meaning "that's not my name and I will not respond".

- Correct – The people I have not known very long and are getting to know, when called out of my name I will correct them with "My name is Timothy!".

- The Look – Most of my good friends, those that are close to me already, know that I hate being called out of my name. So, when they slip up and call me out of my name I give them the *I know you didn't* look. An apology is quickly followed and we then move on.

I don't even let the presumed characteristics of my zodiac sign of Cancer box me in. Whenever someone says *Oh, you are a Cancer,* I always respond with, *that's what they say!*

In the words of Lisa Nicholas, who is a New York Times best-selling author, motivational speaker or as she likes to refer to herself as a "transformational life coach", *you have to teach people how to treat you.* I follow Lisa on YouTube and love her videos that are uploaded quite often. I am not a fan of people trying to place a label on me or put me into a box or a category of their liking. There is a Bible verse that I love that is located in James 3:5. The book of James is my favorite because it is not lengthy and is a good read in the new testament; it is located towards the back of the Bible. That particular verse speaks about the power of the tongue and it says, "In the same way the tongue is a small thing that makes grand speeches but a tiny spark can set a great forest on fire" (New Living Translation Version). The tongue is the most powerful member of our body. How are you using yours? Are you building those around you up with it through positive words? Are you speaking life into situations that are dying or are dead? Not everything requires a response from you either. There have been plenty of times when I've sat back and listened as those around me go back and forth cursing, debating, calling each other out of their name while I say nothing. Sometimes saying nothing is more powerful than any statement you can ever verbally make. Someone is always watching and listening to you, ALWAYS! I remember someone telling me that as soon as you step outside of your house you are on display, on stage, on a platform, and people are watching.

I love stories that you can share out of real-life experiences, so here is a short story for you! This past summer, I went to a local theater here in Atlanta to attend the musical, *The Color Purple*. When I arrived, I walked through the doors and proceeded straight to the Will Call window to retrieve my ticket. It was a ticket that I had purchased months in advance because I knew how popular the show was and how quickly tickets sell out to shows of this caliber. As I approached the counter, the beautiful dark-skinned woman working the Will Call said, "Hi Timothy, we have several people here from out of town trying to see the show tonight. Would you be willing to give up your seat this evening and return on another night?". I paused for a few seconds, looked her in the eyes and replied, "Sure, I can do that". Her face lit up as she called a manager over to inform him that a seat had just became available. The manager then told her that one seat would not matter because the show was about to begin and to just let me in to enjoy the show. She gave me a free drink voucher for my kind gesture. As I gladly accepted it, I told her that the voucher was a nice birthday gift. She was surprised and said that she normally gave a drink voucher to people on their birthdays. She then blessed me with another drink voucher! Whoo Hooo! I was set, a drink before the show and one at intermission; and both were FREE! I then headed off to my seat and took a minute to check out my surroundings. To my left was the sound guy and to my right was an older white lady. During the entire first act she seemed to be annoyed with me. You see, I am very vocal during musicals; to me if a musical doesn't touch every emotion it just wasn't good enough. A musical should touch your soul and leave you with quite an experience. When I watch a musical, it should provoke me to think, laugh, smile, and cry. If you have ever been to a good musical you know what I am describing. In spite of the older lady being annoyed with me, I was enjoying every moment of the show. By intermission, my pre-show drink I'd enjoyed had me wanting to head straight to the bathroom to empty my bladder. Lord knows I had been trying not to piss on myself for a good six musical numbers. *MOVE people*, was all I thought in my head as I hauled ass to the restroom to relieve myself. While I was draining the lizard, I thought about how I was annoying the old lady and felt a bit vexed about it. I began to reason within myself to go back into the second half of the show with a different vibe. I wanted her to enjoy the show and not be irritated by my hooping, hollering and sing-a-longs. Like I said before, a good musical will make you feel it and I have no problem expressing those feelings!

After my bathroom stop, I revisited the bar for my second complimentary cocktail then proceeded back to my seat. The old lady had not returned to hers yet but the sound guy was back and positioned behind his sound board. As soon as I sat down he got my attention with his positive projected words, *YOU ARE GIVING ME LIFE!* Baby when I tell you every thought I had about calming down, being more civilized, sitting back and just enjoying the show went clean out of the window at that moment – it surely did! I was going to be myself and enjoy the show. Sometimes people need just that little reminder to be yourself regardless of what others think, say or assume. I continued the second half of the musical just as the first, screaming "Sing Latrice!". The sound guy even asked me if I was friends with Latrice because I kept screaming her name. Latrice Pace is a well-known gospel artist and I did not personally know her but am a fan. I continued singing along, clapping and of course my well-known loved and hated laugh was present. I was really enjoying myself but the old lady to my right was still annoyed with me. She turned her nose up the entire time, placing her left hand to the side of her face as if she wanted to block the peripheral view of me, which was not working too well. Her body language expressed how uncomfortable she was sitting next to an animated guy who loved musicals.

The stage lights dimmed after the cast took their final bows signifying that this wonderful musical was over. The show was worth every penny spent on the ticket. As we started to head towards the street exit there were at least five people who stopped me to tell me how they loved how I knew all of the lyrics, how they enjoyed my energy and how they were watching me all the way from the other side of the theater. That made my night and affirmed what I had shared earlier. Whether you are in public, at work or in the company of people you know or don't know, always remember that you are a show, a message, a statement and an example. It's up to you if that will be a negative or positive impact. Are you that person who also lives by this? If so, then keep being that person regardless of what anyone else thinks about you because not everyone will understand, like you or be comfortable around you. FUCK THEM!

From this day forward when you step out of the house, when you are at that picnic, at that bar, party, concert or even just walking down the street I want you to ask yourself a few questions. Ask yourself what type of example you are emanating and what are people saying about you when you are not around. I also want to remind you to be very careful with what you allow to influence you through sound and sight. Who and what we allow to influence us shapes who we are as people. I am a huge fan of motivational speakers, affirmations and positive quotes because they empower me to achieve success. I'm also a fan of informative and good self-help books. Have you read any lately? If not, I highly recommend going to Amazon and purchasing *Do Something New* by Shunda Brown; it's an easy read and one of the reasons I was inspired to write this book. Shunda and I have a mutual friend in New York Times Best-Selling author JL King. He has been a huge motivation, inspiration, and helping hand as I took this journey with writing this book. JL is not just an author, but a publisher of plenty of books and is most famous for writing the book *On the Down Low* which landed him with several guest appearances on the Oprah Winfrey show because of the book's eye opening and very informative subject. The book talks about men who live on the downlow with same-sex attractions. If you have not read it, you should.

There is an old church saying that says "ain't no glory without a story". My life hasn't been all peaches and cream, smooth sailing, or a walk in the park. I mean who has a perfect life anyway? Those who do claim to have a perfect life are far and few between and you most likely may never come across them. There is always something to stress you; from bills, to housing trouble, job or career issues, neighbors getting on your nerves, the husband or wife issue and Lord help you if you have children and or pet problems as well. I was fortunate to have been encouraged quite often by close friends. One of the biggest supporters has been my mother, Deborah Keys, who has encouraged me to write my story and share it with you. I will never forget that evening when I was on the phone with my mom and telling her that JL King had informed me he was about to stop publishing books. That was when I was inspired for just a second to write a book. When I opened my mouth to tell my mom of my aspirations to become a published author she was excited as all get out! The words "You should do it!" flew out of her mouth with enthusiasm. After days of pondering the idea, speaking of it to several close people in my circle and putting it into the universe, I continued to get the same feedback – START WRITING!

My book, *I Don't Want to Be That*, will reveal some of my deepest darkest secrets and things I have not shared with anyone. Each chapter heading will reference a song that highlights the message of that chapter. I am no longer going to be ashamed, frightened nor hide from my past. I will expose those things that I saw, the mistakes I made and those wrong roads traveled that transformed me into the man I am today. It's time to tell my story, to reflect on and even rebuke myself for past actions. Sometimes we must openly rebuke ourselves as it is written in Proverbs 27:5, "Open rebuke is better than secret love". My prayer is that by sharing my stories I may open the eyes of readers in similar situations and provide them with hope, courage and inspiration for a way out or to rebuke or confront their situation head on without fear. I went from looking at and being around people that had no hope, was always negative and felt they would never make it in life, to now seeing and having the honor and privilege of being surrounded by entrepreneurs, educators, authors, artists, singers, dancers, actors, actresses and even a few celebrities. I'm surrounded by people who are actually living and loving life, making an impact and having their voices heard. Life can be a wonderful thing if you choose to live, speak and act on things you want to accomplish while here on this earth. Now all that remains is, will you do it?

Chapter 2: "Boondocks"

Song by Little Big Town 2005

I was born sometime in the wee hours of the morning of July 9, 1981 in Opelousas, Louisiana. Opelousas means flathead catfish which my hometown was known to have in abundance for local fishermen. This is where this little Louisiana boy's story begins. My parents, Deborah and Al, were just two middle class people in love trying to make ends meet, we all know how that is. I am their middle child of three. My sister was born seven years earlier in 1974 and my brother arrived after me in 1983. The earliest childhood memories were when we lived in a trailer near the railroad tracks. I recall the many times we had to walk across those tracks to "make groceries" for mom at the bread store. Now in case you didn't know, down in Louisiana we make groceries – you better ask somebody! In places like New York City corner stores are called bodegas, down where I am from we call them the bread store. Every region has its own way of speaking and ours were unique.

My brother and I would play outside with dead frogs, catch bees and remove one of their wings and watch them buzz around in circles. We got a lot of bee stings doing that, but it never stopped us. Mud pies? Yep we made them. Dragon flies? Yep we chased them. Crawfish? You bet ya bottoms we were in that muddy water grabbing them suckers with our bare hands. I had so much fun during that time although I don't recall many memories with my sister while we lived in that trailer. I just remember a story my mom had shared with me at an older age about something wild my sister had done. Apparently, she had set a decorative plant on fire with a lighter she was playing with and that antic almost took my life. I was an infant napping on the couch and was almost left there to burn in that trailer, BUT GOD!

The earliest memories I do recall interacting with my sister were mainly of us fighting. We were always going at it. I don't know what it was but my younger brother and I were cool but she and I always had beef with each other. She would always hide the phone from me or lock me out of the house for hours until I would get fed up to the point of searching for something high enough to climb on in order to gain entrance through the front window of the house that led to her bedroom. One time she and I were having one of our fights and her best friend tried helping her by jumping into the middle of it. I was a feisty little fella and I didn't want to stop which is why her friend tried to help her. I wanted blood and had my legs wrapped around her neck. Both of my little caramel colored hands were filled with her light red hair. As my sister's friend approached, she grabbed my arm in an attempt to get me to turn my sister's hair loose. Well, that was a big mistake because seconds later the heel of my cowboy boot was introduced to her forehead, she then backed away. Once I did manage to turn her loose, I ran into the kitchen and went straight into the drawer for a knife. My sister followed me and stormed into the kitchen thinking she was about to take me down. Before she knew what was happening, that knife came from behind my back and was held to her stomach. I could feel myself pushing it in about to break skin, then I heard mom's car pull up into the carport. My sister was a lucky ass that day because I was about to send her straight to the hospital's emergency room. For some reason, my sister was a mean bully. I recall a day when there was nothing but wire hangers being thrown around in the house. Now did she throw them at mom or did mom throw them at her? All I remember was I really wanted to kick her ass; but then I was too young and would have lost that battle big time. I thank God that today my sister and I are really good friends and love to be in the presence of one another. Time and maturity helped to heal our old wounds and now I would beat somebody's ass if they tried to mess with her.

Opelousas was a small populated town that still had plenty of dirt and gravel roads. It was here that I began to see and comprehend things going on around me. I began to see things around me that I didn't want to be, but they served as a guidepost and determination for me not to become them. These were the things that made me say *I don't want to be that.* This small town was my birthplace and my humble beginning, but it was also the motivation for a better life. I saw and remember my aunts and uncles as grown ass adults still living under one roof with their mom (my grandmother or as we would say in Louisiana, "Momo"). I didn't want that to be me! I truly believe that was one of the first times I said that to myself out loud, and I was very young. I knew at that age that I wanted independence when I became an adult with my own place of residence.

There were many things that I was exposed to while growing up in Opelousas. I remember as a young child being introduced to alcohol and cigarettes by my uncle. I can still recall him teaching me to take a puff, blow out the smoke and then drink a sip of beer. Giving alcohol to children was no biggie to him and some of our other family members. When we had a fever, trust me a shot of whiskey was in our near future. Videos of women being penetrated by horses and other pornography were proudly shown to me as a young child by my uncle. He wasn't my blood uncle, but more like the man who was shacking up with my aunt. Although they weren't married we still called him our uncle out of respect. My aunt would lite a cigarette for him with it still in her mouth, she'd then take it out and call me over to have me walk it over to him. Although these were not good childhood memories, I had many that were very good. Today, I live my life in a manner that has more than made up for the bad memories. I enjoy life and treating those I care for with goodness. Still till this day, my mom can be heard on the other end of the phone line during one of our conversations asking things like *You paid how much for those shoes?* or *The plane ticket was that expensive?* If I treat her out for her birthday she may say something like, *So, it cost that much for this little steak, you don't need to spend that much money.* I may not be rich and may still have to ask my mom for money here and there, but I hope to never look at situations in that way as if I

18

am not deserving of the best. No, I am not throwing my mom under the bus by saying this either. I'm just giving you some examples of why I repeat the mantra, *I don't want to be that.* If we are celebrating a birthday I plan on having a great time and spend money or we are not doing anything at all. My family did not have much growing up, which is the reason I wanted more out of life and why my mom is the way she is, I get it. I wanted to see the world, purchase that $40 steak to taste the difference between how that restaurant's medium rare steak tasted versus the cheap home and over cooked pepper steak that was served to us with rice and gravy while growing up. Please do not get it twisted though, I am a country Louisiana boy through and through and still love me some good ole pepper steak!

Thankfully, my dad had a job about sixty miles east of Opelousas in the city of Baton Rouge. The city's name is of French origin and translates into meaning red stick. Baton Rouge is the capital of Louisiana. Yep you read that correctly, sorry to burst your bubble, but New Orleans is NOT the capital. Eventually we moved there and settled in Easy Town, or as we use to spell it EZ Town, a small known urban hood. Though not too far from downtown, and the campus of LSU (Louisiana State University), it wasn't the best nor the safest location in the east Baton Rouge parish. On any given corner you could find a stop sign tagged with "EZ TOWN" in white spray paint. Every Sunday just down the street from our home was basically a ghetto car parade going on. All of these old cars would be lined up on Gus Young Avenue, blasting music while proudly sporting their hydraulics, which I am sure caused them some body aches. There were lots of dancing, fighting and shooting happening on Sundays during the time those cars overtook that street. Until this day my mom still lives in that little two-bedroom wooden house that sits on a corner in Easy Town. The house is shaded by the leaves of the two huge oak trees, one in the front yard and one on the side. I will never forget that old, ugly, yellow abandoned store across the street from us. It looked like one of those old storefronts you see in the movies with the attendant sitting in front waiting to assist you when you arrived. There was an abundance of drug deals that went down right there on that corner. My little brother and I saw plenty of drug transactions going on in front of that old store. The city, state government or somebody eventually had it torn down. Although that store had been out of business for God knows how long, it didn't stop the dealers and dope fiends from doing their transactions. Fortunately, it did slow down the traffic passing directly in front of our house.

My brother and I spent many nights on pallets in the middle of the living room floor in fear for our lives. A good ole drive by or two happened regularly. After the gun shots would cease, my brother and I would crawl on our hands and knees down the hall to our parents' bedroom to check on mom. Why was it always our mom that we were concerned about or wanted to check on? Did we not care to see if dad was okay or was it that we looked at him as a superhuman? As the years went on, so did the shootings, break-ins, robberies, theft of car batteries and of course the neighborhood fights and so forth. I guess being in that area rubbed off on me a little. I did not let things go as easy, had a temper if you pissed me off and would be ready to fight in a heartbeat. Okay, I will admit that I was a little ratchet and didn't give a fuck unlike my sister, who was afraid to have a scratch on her face. If my friends and I were playing pencil pop (remember that game?) and someone actually broke my pencil, guess what? You had better be ready for a good ole fashion Louisiana street fight. I mean we would be seriously going at it in the middle of the street, fists up, shoes off, friends in a circle egging on the fight and cheering for the one they wanted to win. That was when fighting was just that, fighting with your fists. As for the younger generation coming up after me there would be more unfair fighting happening. They'd bring weapons to their fights. During the time my friends and I were in middle school, we'd be fighting until we were rolling in the dirt. We wouldn't stop until the fight was broken up by the parents or neighbors. Those were some memories! After about ten years or so of living in that hood, in that house, on that corner, in Easy Town, we knew everyone and they knew us. When we would leave to go out of town to visit family or take a vacation the neighbors would keep an eye on the house for us. Those neighbors included the thugs and drug dealers, whom we became really close to and trusted that they'd make sure our home was safe. My family had become complacent and comfortable in that rough part of town, but in the back of my head I still wanted OUT!

My brother and I were actually really well known to the point of being recognized by others with just the hearing of our nicknames. My brother's nickname was Julio, due to his fair skin complexion and wavy hair, mine was Professor. I was known for sitting on the front steps reading a book or doing homework instead of playing, going bike riding or participating in play activities with the other local children. I mean I had fun during my youth, but I have always been the more serious person or at least in my eyes I was. You would always find me talking with or hanging out with people older than myself. I guess that is why I always looked at things differently and kept my eyes open. As early as my teens, I recall watching the Weather Channel as well as the Real Estate Channel. I wanted to get the hell out of Baton Rouge so bad I guess seeing the weather and housing in different places was my way of a temporary escape. It gave me ideas of where I would like to relocate when the time came. I have to admit though that my teen years were great. In high school I did a little bit of everything. I was a proud member of Capitol High School, which was blocks away from where we lived. I was voted best school spirit, most likely to succeed and most courteous for three of the four years attending that school. Yes, believe it or not I was voted most courteous – the one who would tussle and fight in the streets when I was a bit younger.

During my four years in high school I was an active member of the Army JROTC (Junior Officer Training Course), and would annually attend the summer boot camp they offered at Camp Beauregard. I will never forget that place; it was located in northern Louisiana in the middle of nowhere. I remember learning to hydrate and eat right. Who knew the body will let you know if you are eating correctly by regular bowel movements? At that time, I sure didn't. We did our company's early morning formations, attendance check, basic roll call, have breakfast and then start the day. Plenty of obstacle courses were completed, zip lining, team building exercises, etc. This camp was located near Shreveport, Louisiana and at night the streets where like a big ass party. The boys in Shreveport were bouncers and booty poppers like in New Orleans. Honey, you better believe I was there for it!

In high school I was also a member of the drill team, color guard, funeral detail and rifle team. I participated in the marching band for a while and my instrument of choice was the trumpet. I was able to carry that talent over to the ROTC program by playing taps at funerals for active soldiers or veterans for a little cash if my services were requested. It wasn't much, but hell back then when I was able to purchase my own super-sized Big Mac meal which was a big deal for me. Those years were special and created great memories. I enjoyed the practices, sweat, tears and those long ass parades we marched in. All of those things still have a special place in my heart. Being that I was so involved with JROTC and the fact that my father had served in the U.S. Army were definitely reasons why I enlisted into the military later in life. The pictures of my dad in South Korea that hung in my parents' bedroom where a constant reminder of his service to the nation.

I enjoyed hearing all of the stories he had shared which inspired as well as motivated me! Yep what my dad had experienced really spoke to me and I wanted to have the same or at least similar stories and memories. I longed to see the world and be well traveled. Unlike my mom, I did not want to be that person that did not travel or be too afraid to fly. Traveling was something I wanted to experience multiple times to different places. My dad was a great man. He was a man I looked up to and was a go-getter and the life of the party. People would often say I remind them of him because I'm the life of the party now. They'd say, "So, that's where you get that from!". Other people who knew my dad, would say, "Boy you just like ya daddy!". Though he was very dark skinned, and I am a lighter complexion, our laugh, love for cooking and entertaining people are things we have in common. Looking back on it now, I would say that my dad was not a complainer. I loved that about him and that quality is what also inspired me to be a more positive person. He would always make the best of every situation no matter how unfortunate the situation may have been or appeared to be. His influence in my life would impact me greatly.

Chapter 3: Is That Your Baby?

Song by Barney: "I Love You" 1993

Life has a way of bringing new experiences to you unexpectedly. It happened for me in 1996 when my niece was born. As a young teenager, no more than fifteen or sixteen years old, I became an uncle for the first time in my life. Although my sister and I had fought a lot, she was always someone I admired and thought was a very smart and a strong-minded human being. She was always ready for a good dance party, hanging out with her friends or going shopping. She lived for these things because she enjoyed life. My sister was the pretty, popular girl with the resting bitch face. Those that did not know her assumed she was mean and unapproachable, but she wasn't. Shortly after graduating high school she set off to attend college which made our family proud. She was accepted to and attended two well-known black historical universities in Louisiana, Southern University, which is in Baton Rouge, and Grambling University, which is about four hours north of Baton Rouge in a small town named after the university itself. She later moved to Houston, Texas which provided a nice escape for me from time to time when I wanted to get away from Baton Rouge.

I will never forget that morning my sister was pacing the floor of the living room while in labor; it was an early morning before I had left the house for school. When a contraction would hit her, she would grab the handle of a nearby doorknob or arm of the sofa to bear down on until it had subsided. Those contractions nearly drew her to her knees in a hunched position. After the contraction she would stand tall, begin pacing again and repeatedly mumble under her breath, "That wasn't that bad". That night after school I proceeded straight to the hospital to see my niece for the first time. From that day forward, I felt like the dad because my little girl, my niece, became my life. Being a young single mom is not easy and I helped my sister out a lot by taking care of and looking after my niece. My sister appreciated the help quite a bit because she needed it. Unfortunately, she missed a lot of her daughter's childhood by leaving her with me so often. I was the one there when her navel scab fell off, the one who was there for her first go on the potty unassisted. I was the one that was there when she took her first step. To keep her busy and happy, the television character Barney was always my default. This is why the Barney theme song, *I Love You*, is referenced for this chapter. This little light skinned beauty was with me everywhere I went; yes, I was her uncle but was also her play-daddy. In the mall with friends, there she was; high school football games, yep I had the baby seat with me there as well. That is why the question "Is that your baby?" was asked so frequently! I could not escape it. She was born in October so at two months, when Christmas time arrived, she accompanied me to a Christmas carol a friend of mine was singing at and that is where she had her first picture with Santa Claus taken. I remember her little

26

fingers squeezing my finger, and how she was bald in the back of her head for the longest. My baby had to be like two years old before she had a full head of hair. Everyone thought she was my child and raising her really matured me fast because I was doing everything a father would do. A friend of mine who lived around the corner from me was in a similar situation with her siblings; but she was ordered by her mom to cook, clean and take care of her younger brothers and sisters. That girl worked hard and I was there with her moving furniture as she would sweep, walking with her to the grocery store or helping her with whatever else she needed. God knows she needed a helping hand and I was there to support my friend.

Chapter 4: "Bill"

Song by Peggy Scott 2007

My mother's side of the family grew up in the local Catholic church in Opelousas, but once we relocated to Baton Rouge we began to attend my dad's family church. His side of the family was very serious about their Christianity. They were members of the COGIC church which stands for the Church of God in Christ. Now honey, let me tell you that was CHURRRCH! Nobody can out shout the COGIC folks!!! Of course, they preached against sex before marriage, homosexuality and drugs, but at the time I was too young to understand or even care for any of those conservative views. I just enjoyed the music, seeing my family and watching people praise God and catch the Holy Ghost. We would attend all of the Bible studies, Sunday school classes, and vacation Bible school where we had learned a lot. This guy Jesus, who in the Bible was the son of God (the creator of the universe, the maker of heaven and earth), fascinated me. As a matter of fact, most of the stories in the Bible fascinated me. I can still remember the lunch times and making t-shirts with water paint during vacation Bible school. Oh, to be a kid again!

One Sunday morning, in ninth grade or so, my sister had decided to visit a non-denominational church. She was now driving on her own by this time and asked me if

I wanted to attend service with her and a friend that next Sunday. I said yes, we got up at around eight in the morning the next Sunday, got ready and left the house to head to service around 9:45 a.m., the drive to the church was about twenty minutes. We wanted to be on time to park and get a good seat because service started at 10:30 a.m. The service was refreshing and something we had never experienced before. From then on out whenever we felt the need to go to a worship service, we attended that church because we loved the come as you are approach. The moment you walked through the doors of the sanctuary, someone was there to welcome you with a smile, hug and or handshake. They made us feel both welcomed and comfortable. As soon as the clock struck 10:30 a.m., the praise and worship would begin and the celebration of our faith would fill the sanctuary. We also loved it because they did everything on time unlike the Baptist church, Church of God in Christ or a few other denominational churches I had visited. Once I learned to drive and had my driver's license I went back and joined that church. I had given my life to Jesus and it was the best feeling in the world. Stacy, a girl I met in high school and I had been dating, began accompanying me to services. It was there, at that church where we prayed together, we cried together, we bonded and grew closer in love with each other and God. We spent a lot of time at that church, especially after joining the youth ministry and convincing many of our friends to join as well. It was a megachurch so it had everything imaginable. There was a game room, basketball court, television room and a restaurant. Seriously, we would go to this church just to hang out with like-minded teens. Other teens would be found at the movies, malls and local skating rinks, while we were at the house of the Lord.

This place of worship, this safe haven, this holy place was not only the place my girlfriend and I went but was also the place I met Jacob. This slim, dark skinned, handsome young man stood about 5'7, which was just a few inches taller than me. He had a great smile and beautiful teeth. He was a hip-hop dancer and instructor and I would sometimes stop by the studio just to see him in his element. When he would notice me, a smile would appear on his face as he twirled so gracefully into his next dance movement. I would sit and watch the sweat roll from his face, down his neck until it would disappear behind his low-cut tank top after traveling between his pecs. He was beautiful to watch. He didn't live too far from the dance studio, but I always insisted on giving him a ride home.

When I was not with my Stacy, I was with Jacob. We were like best friends in the eyes of everyone else. What people didn't know was that Jacob was my little secret, lover and first real boyfriend. During Sunday services, he would be sitting on my left side and Stacy would be on my right. Yes, we were all friends and were close, but she nor anyone else knew about the secret relationship between Jacob and me. We would praise God together during church service on Sunday morning, then that night while in bed we would listen to the song *If They Only Knew*. As we listened to the song we would sing along, hold each other and cry because we knew and felt what we had and what we were doing was wrong according to the Bible and church. The song was by

Trinitee 5:7, which at the time was a very popular female gospel group. Well after the tears dried and the songs ended, the guilt would flee and we would make love. Even then sometime a tear would fall from his eye while we were in the middle of having sex. Behind closed doors Jacob and I were very passionate towards one another. I thought we would be together for a long time, there were many nights I cried myself to sleep thinking of him while trying to pray. Sometimes my conflict felt unbearable.

Chapter 5: "He Proposed to Me"

Song by Kelly Price 2003

Stacy and I had just started dating in 1997. Both of us were, I believe, juniors in high school. We did love each other very much and our relationship lasted for two full years. She was my friend, my rock, my prayer partner and my lover. For me, those two years were hell on earth because I had two beautiful people in my life that loved me and I loved them which made me feel unsettled inside. As we became more involved with the church, I tried to shake the feelings I had deep down inside and quickly became a cell leader. In megachurches the congregation is huge (over 3,000 members) and is believed to be the body of Christ. With so many members, and in order to minister efficiently so that no member felt left out, cell groups were formed. This group would meet at a location and have Bible study. The cell groups were organized based on zip codes and you'd meet there for convenience. We, the cell group, would take turns having the meetings at each other's houses. Snacks would also be provided and we would begin each meeting with praise and worship followed by an opening prayer.

I became that guy everyone looked up to and sought after for prayer and/or advice. You could notice me from across the church indulged in radical praise. I would shout in a heartbeat or take off running across the church in the blink of an eye. Little did they know though after the services, praise dancing, shouting and falling under the anointing, I was sleeping with Jacob; the guy that was by my side shouting and praising along with me. We were so involved in the church that in 1999, we did not attend our high school senior year prom because we had chosen to attend our church's prom instead. The church had a MORP for us, which was prom spelled backwards. MORP is a casual dance where the girls ask the guys to dance or attend. Even though there was no dance at ours, we went to dinner and they took us to see some cheesy ass animated movie. Yeah it was so horrible I can't even recall the name. In spite of that, it still was a perfect night, the night I had plans to propose to Stacy. God, I remember the day my mom and I went to Walmart to pick out and purchase that cheap ass ring I was going to give to her. If I remember correctly the ring was $99 before taxes, it was cute though. I was in high school and we were working at an amusement park called Fun Fair Park as ride operators, so that was the best I could do at the time. So, don't judge me! I was nervous but ready. Our friends were over at my mom's house for the big moment. I had written a twelve-line poem, had a dozen of red roses, the ring and a pillow. I was in my bedroom with my eleven friends who each had a rose and a line to the poem to recite. On the other side of my bedroom door was my mom and a friend that was going to sing.

When Stacy and her family arrived, my friend began to sing what I believe was Whitney Houston's song *I Will Always Love You*. It was so long ago I'm not too sure it was that song but I believe it was. Once they began the song it was the queue for my friends with the roses and lines to the poem to begin to come out and do their thing. One by one my friends came out of my room and entered the living area where Stacy stood in a beautiful blue evening gown with not a hair out of place. A rose was placed in her hand as they recited their assigned line from the poem. The eleventh rose had been given and the eleventh line had been recited. I was the last to go in with the finale. With my hands sweating, and heart racing, I came out, threw the pillow on the floor, got on one knee and asked for her hand in marriage. There was not a dry eye in the house as she said yes, but in my mind, I was thinking, *What the fuck are you doing? You're in love with a man.*

Chapter 6: "I'm Coming Out"

Song by Diana Ross 1980

You know how the church preaches no sex before marriage? Well how many folks really love hearing that sermon? We were young and curious, and by all means if we were going to be together for a long time, we needed to know if the sex would be good. We convinced Stacy's older sister to get us a hotel room and were planning a night of romance and passionate love making. The hotel was right downtown, near the levee, which is a waterfront if you are not familiar. Stacy and I were planning to get married for God's sake, He will forgive us, right? I remember arriving and entering the room to see Stacy in bed with a pretty white satin girly thing on, and smelling like straight up Johnson and Johnson. Yeah, baby power was her thing. I gave her a kiss then proceeded to shower and PRAY! The intent was to come out and make love to this dark-skinned beauty and be made whole, become even more in love with her and have a taste of what it was like to be inside of a female. Well after I got out of the shower...that was the end of all of that because nothing happened. Who was I fooling because I could not get hard and could only think of Jacob. I believe that boy had roots on me! Just joking but I mean we are from Louisiana where hoodoo and voodoo are not uncommon practices.

Weeks later, Stacy was still upset and crying over what happened that night. I hated to see her upset and couldn't take it anymore, I could not keep her in pain. She felt it was all her fault, that she had done something wrong or she was not attractive to me. Wanting to free her from this torment in her mind, I had to tell her the truth. In the form of a letter, I explained why that night my member would not work. One night I went by her apartment and sat next to her on the sofa, handed her the letter and began to pray. Stacy was from right outside of New Orleans, had been a gang member and had gold teeth in her mouth. I was dating her at the time the song *Thug Girl* by Master P and Snoop Dogg was out and one of the song lyrics was "I need a thug girl" and I had one. I was about 5'3 weighing 110 lbs., WET! She could have easily kicked my ass so I wasn't too sure what her reaction would be to me coming out to her. That night was rough, we cried and held each other for hours after she read the letter. I came out to her about my sexuality and had let her know about the relationship I had with Jacob. We still love one another until this very day. The church helped me to form close friendships with others I am still in contact with even now. I thank God Stacy didn't reject me as her friend or made me feel bad for opening up to her as a gay man. Coming out to her had set me free to now live my truth and I am grateful to her for making it easier. I was freed! It felt like being released from a prison and free to live my life.

Now I wanted and felt a need to come out of the closet to everyone. I had to tell my mom that although I was a converted church boy, I was gay, a homosexual. Although

I felt liberated, I still wondered how was I going to tell my mom and what would be her reaction. I had so many questions including when should I do it, what was the best time and would she reject me. So many questions, concerns and fears filled my head and heart. What helped? Well I was no longer seeing Jacob because we had decided after a long talk and cry we could not continue our relationship. We parted ways around the time I thought I wanted to get married to Stacy. After coming out to Stacy, I began to hang out at the local gay clubs and bars. One night at a little hole in the wall, I had met this older, cute, white guy from a small country town. We ended up dating for a few months. He had a country accent with a sweet personality and lived in a trailer with a snake. Shortly after dating him, I met another guy, a baker named Carl. During this time, my mom was still moaning, crying and complaining about the breakup between Stacy and me. She was crying one evening and began questioning me, *Why this, Why that, I thought she was going to be my daughter-n-law, What happened?, Ya'll were perfect together!* That's when I pulled out a picture of Carl, and yes, a printed photo, held it up to her face and said **"HE IS WHY!"** It wasn't quite the way I had planned on coming out to her, but it happened nonetheless. All of this took place in 1999, the summer after I graduated from high school. Mom took it hard at first, blaming herself, but it got better with time. After coming out I was exposed to all the gay bars, clubs and cruising spots in Baton Rouge and surrounding areas. Those days were fun, all I did was party and go to the mall, movies, coffee shops, cyber cafes and hang out with friends. I went through many stages of trying to figure out who I was in the LGBTQ (Lesbian, Gay, Bisexual, Transgender, Queer) community. Because our community is so rejected by mainstream society, this trying to figure out where you fit in is not uncommon. It's hard enough being gay, but being a gay black man in the conservative Bible belt part of the country makes it even tougher. I didn't care though, it was my life and I was living it on my terms.

Chapter 7: "Brokenhearted"

By: Brandy featuring Wanya Morris 1994

Can I tell you something? Well I feel like at this point, I can tell you anything because I have already began spitting out all of my tea to you anyway. So, I had a crush on a boy in the neighborhood named Kyle and he felt the same about me. We began to act on that crush and started messing around with each other. I always knew as far back as I can remember that I was attracted to guys. I did not want to have those feelings at first and tried to fight them off because I was conditioned to believe that this was not normal and people frowned down on gays. Kyle was a dark chocolate guy that not only lived around the corner but we also went to elementary school together. Whenever we would spend nights at each other's home we would play around, taking turns touching each other and exploring one another's bodies. The older we got the more we did and experimented with during our sexual encounters. This went on until after high school, he was a friend with benefits and I liked it. I liked his family and I can still hear his dad's voice telling me *You going to have high blood pressure,* when I would go to town with the salt on my pork chops, rice, gravy and corn. His family was sweet and loved having me over as a guest in their home. We would always take a bath, get in our pajamas and have dinner together before bed.

41

Then he and I would freak one another under the covers on the pallet that was prepared for us on the floor. It was fun.

After high school, and me coming out, I would see him here and there and we'd hook up for sex. Each time was a little different and I noticed things about him were changing. For example, his approach and his look were different. He was going down a wrong road and I could see it, but I had such a connection with him that I wouldn't say anything and would occasionally give him the money he requested for him sucking me off. I would see him walking Plank Road, which was the street most hookers walked along with the trade, drug dealers and hustlers. I remember Kyle asking me one night if I wanted to make some money, I jumped at the opportunity before even thinking. One should never do this! He got into the car and provided me with directions to this apartment complex not far away. After finding a parking space, we then walked up a flight of stairs to some guy's place, the door was unlocked and we let ourselves in. Kyle went to the back towards the man's bedroom to talk with him for a minute while I sat in the living room on the couch. I was nervous as shit. Kyle returns to tell me what I had to do to receive payment and after hearing what he had to say I wanted no part of it. He wanted me to participate in a threesome with this older 300-pound white guy. I could not and would not do that, so I told him to go make his money and I would wait for him. Shortly after this awkward situation occurred I hooked up with Kyle one more time. After he left I realized this motherfucker had taken an old phone and one of my pagers from me. Oh, please tell me you know what a pager is, a beeper? Hell, look it up if you don't know! I recall looking around for those missing items and saying to myself, *never again.* This relationship had been ongoing for years and I was brokenhearted that he had done that to me. Realizing what the love of money, drugs and sex could do to a person had me saying once again that *I don't want to be that!* I believe that Bible scripture in 1 Timothy 6:10 which says, "For the love of money is a root of kinds of evil. Some people, eager for money, have wandered from the fait and pierced themselves with many griefs."

Chapter 8: "It Gets Better"

Song by: Todrick Hall 2010

The year after I graduated from high school felt like forever, everything just seemed to move in slow motion. Maybe it was because I did so much and didn't sleep much. It was if I did not want to miss out on anything. I attended a community college for a short period of time, the school was fairly new and just five minutes away from where I lived. It was a small campus situated in the middle of a parking lot behind a local McDonald's restaurant. It was technically a campus but not much of one. The school had only one building filled with classes, a bookstore and the enrollment office. I had met a guy at the school, Dave, whom I had a crush on. Before classes started in the morning we would meet at that McDonald's for breakfast and I would always get a bacon and egg McGriddle with extra hash browns. Dave was about 5'10, light complexion with beautiful dark wavy hair that was always perfectly faded. He had a smile that would brighten up anyone's day. We always had great conversations as we enjoyed our food and each other's company. Sitting across from the table from him at that McDonald's, I remember sharing with him the struggle I was having with being gay and trying to live my life as a Christian. In return he shared his story about being attracted to the same sex as well. We started to hang out together and, in my head, I was in love with him.

Dave was a hairstylist and an inspiration to me. I began to picture myself as a stylist too although I had not made it too serious of a thought at the time, but I could picture it. Dave was an older guy, maybe about seven to ten years my senior which in the gay community isn't a whole lot older than you. He would come by the house to visit and we would sit in his car and kiss, that's about as far as we went though. The irony is he was the stylist that did my mom's hair for my graduation so I had actually met him while I was still in high school. Sometime between the breakup with Stacy and before I met Carl was when we had met at a club. Dave was in my life during that time I was struggling in church and trying to reconcile my faith with who I was as a gay man. I believe that is why we ended up having that heart to heart while attending community college together. He knew the concerns of my heart and I trusted him enough to share them.

Straight male friends? Although heterosexual males can be toxic as hell towards gay men, I still had them as friends and fortunately for me they still wanted to hang which made me feel good. Do you know how many LGBTQ people lose friends when they come out to them? Trust me, it happens quite a bit so I was fortunate. Some of my straight friends would trip just a little. There were a few that would look at me funny when we were left in a room alone. It wasn't that they were rejecting me, honey let me tell you it was quite the opposite. I would look them in the eyes and say "We both want the same thing, to get our dicks wet, so stop looking at me like that, I don't want you!". Some straight guys do not like to be close to, around or friends with gay guys. They honestly believe we may want them just because they have a dick. They think like this because of a lack of knowledge about gays or are not around a lot of us. Unlike some gay guys I didn't try sleeping with every straight, down low, bisexual or trade male I found attractive. Once I told them I was not like that, all was well and we were cool.

If you're not familiar with some of the terminology used within the LGBTQ community let me share with you what I mean by "trade". According to the Urban Dictionary the term trade is a straight guy that lets or allows a gay man to perform oral sex on him. Hell, I was the one wanting oral sex performed on me so we could do nothing for each other anyway which is why I didn't seek out trade. Some of my friends were so cool with it though. Some of those straight friends came to gay clubs with me and others would stand over me in straight clubs like bodyguards just in case someone tried to mess with me. I knew my mother had become accustomed and comfortable with my homosexuality the day she had asked a lover of mine about our sex life. That let me know right there that she was a little more than comfortable with me being gay! I never asked her why because I didn't care, but I assumed because in her head I was "the man" in the relationship and my partner was more of the role of "the woman". Of course, we were both men, but you know most straight people are clueless of gay culture. We were both men and proud of it. One of my ex-lovers broke it down to her and let her know that I was the giver and he was the receiver.

There you have it, my mom discovered that in some gay relationships it consists of a top and a bottom. Don't get it twisted either, just because a guy is very masculine acting doesn't mean he's exclusively the giver (top). There are very masculine men who prefer being bottoms and some feminine men who prefer being the tops. You cannot assume who is who by just looking at them. Mom was relieved that I did not desire to be a woman or had any interest in dressing in drag (women's clothing, shoes, wigs, underwear, etc.). She had become very cool with a lot of my boyfriends and was always asking questions and learning more about the LGBTQ community. This was very important for me and if you have someone in your life that is gay or bi-curious please talk to them and educate yourself. They will be more than happy to educate you on the diversity of our community. On my book cover you saw the word "faggot". I did not want to be called or labeled this in any way. That word does mean a male homosexual but when used by most people it is intended to be offensive. I am a proud gay man, not a faggot. Just as the word nigger means a black or dark-skinned person and is meant to be offensive, so is the word faggot. You do not have to believe me and you can disagree all day every day. Go ahead and look those two words up. They are nouns that both say are offensive; remember that a noun is used to identify any of a class of people, places, or things. We have all heard that knowledge is power, so go and gain some power, do a little research about that guy you are afraid to sit next to at the football game because he is gay, or that woman you are scared to hug at the community meet and greet because she's a lesbian. These are forms of homophobia and it is rooted in fear and ignorance.

This is why we must learn about what we're ignorant of in life. Learning means knowledge acquired through experience, study, or being taught. If you do not seek, research, or inquire you will never learn. So, go to the library and check out some books about gay culture; have an in-depth chat with that gay guy in your neighborhood or at your workplace asking him questions so that you can get answers. Just don't assume, ask. They are human beings, just like you. We all bleed, breath and live on earth with each other. It's time to stop the pointing, condemning and chastising because something makes you uncomfortable. It's time to start learning more about these people we share space with on this planet. Trust me, gay people aren't going anywhere and we've been on this earth for thousands of years. Think about how you treat someone who is disabled, was recently diagnosed with a disease, has a deformity or is of another nationality. You would likely treat them with respect or want to get to know them better as a human being. Stop calling LGBTQ people derogatory names. Just as that "little person" that has dwarfism and may prefer to be referred to by their name or as a "person of short stature" versus as a dwarf, honor the humanity in LGBTQ people as well. I bet you had never thought of those things from that perspective, have you? Hopefully, now when you see something unfamiliar you will be led to do a little digging to find out just a little more about whatever it is that caught your inquiring eye.

"The ultimate ignorance is the rejection of something you know nothing about, yet refuse to investigate"
Dr. Wayne Dyer

"Ignorance is never better than knowledge."
Enrico Fermi

"The ignorant are ignorant of their ignorance."
Peter Baskerville

"Living is easy with eyes closed."
John Lennon

Chapter 9: "Changed"

Gospel Song by Tramaine Hawkins 2001

One of the early jobs I had was with the Department of Labor which was across the street from my high school and walking distance from where I lived. I enjoyed working there and the experience was amazing. One of the reasons I enjoyed it so much was due to my supervisor, Ms. Dee, who became a second mother to me. Within months she was also my mentor and achieved the position of my spiritual mother. We attended the same church and would sometimes do some fun things together. I'd often sit with her during church service, but not always. She was hard of hearing and would often sit in the first or second row so that she could either read lips or be near the sign language interpreter. I didn't always sit that close to the front. Ms. Dee was and is to this present day my heart, rock and someone I can go to when I need to talk, in need of prayer or a good laugh or cry. She was and is like a best friend and we have a lot of memories together.

In 2016 Ms. Dee came to Atlanta for a visit and stayed with me. During her visit we attended the free annual Atlanta Jazz Festival at Piedmont Park, which is a well-known and frequently visited urban park. The park was within walking distance from my apartment. There is always something fun to do here in Atlanta which is why a lot of people I know enjoy coming here to visit me. One day, while at work, I came out to Ms. Dee as a gay man. I had expressed to her my struggle with my sexuality and the church. That same week she gifted me a small canvas with an image of a cat, she knew how much I loved cats. The words on the canvas read, "A friend is someone who knows all about you and still loves you just the same". That just brought me to tears! The tears began to just drop from my eyes. You know those big heavy fat tear drops that don't even run down your face, they just fall. Yep, those tears were falling: No straight person will ever understand how hard coming out is for a person in the LGBTQ community. We fear rejection, and in some cases, possible bodily harm and violence. The fact is some become homeless, beaten and or even killed for coming out. We are looked at as less than human, a sinner, a disappointment even. Who wants that stigma? That's why many prefer to stay closeted. What if everyone you knew were gay but you liked the opposite sex? How comfortable would you be telling your two dads or two moms that you were straight and not gay like them? You were that thing the pastor preached hell's fire against. Not easy to imagine right?

After sharing my truth to Ms. Dee, we became even closer and would talk about everything. She would tell me how she would pray to God and one of her prayers was simple, *Lord, I just want some sex!* Her honesty was delightful, refreshing, appreciated and needed. Ms. Dee would always tell me "He, God, is your father you should be able to talk to him just like your earthly father". Well I didn't really talk to my earthly father like that, but I understood the message she was sharing with me. One day I confessed to her that I had been masturbating to a gay porn magazine and I needed to repent and throw it away. She agreed with me, but told me first I had to bring it to her so she could look at it. I WAS TOO DONE!! That was Ms. Dee, very spiritual but real as hell. Unlike most Christians or should I say church folk, she was a person I could share anything with and not be judged or looked at differently. Even the Bible talks about not judging others in Matthew 7:1 which says "Judge not, that ye be not judged". I feel like a true Christian truly lives by the word of God and does not judge, instead they pray with and for you. I still refer to her as mom. Ms. Dee and my mother became good friends as well which was nice to see happen. I remember when Ms. Dee and my mom took a trip with a group of women to go see Bishop T.D. Jakes in Atlanta for the *Woman Thou Art Loose* conference. I wanted my mom to experience the presence of God like Ms. Dee and I had on so many occasions at church and other events. Ms. Dee and I had been to so many gospel music concerts, church services, revivals and had even traveled to go see some famous ministers. The sermons, messages and stories heard throughout those years touched me. The people I met and the things I saw really opened my eyes even more with how to become a better person. My thoughts began to change and the way I talked began to become more positive. I was evolving and changing. Back then, there was a popular gospel song that I would cry to every time I heard it, most good gospel songs have that effect on me. Tramaine Hawkins I believe is who came out with the song called *Changed* that rapidly hit the choir stands of most churches. The lyrics to the song are so beautiful:

A wonderful change has come over me

A wonderful change has come over me

Lord you've changed

Changed

You've changed my life complete

Changed

And now I sit

Changed

I sit at the Saviour's feet.

If you haven't heard this song I strongly encourage you to at least listen to it one time and then try to change something about your life or circumstance. Even if it's just one thing, just try it. Changing who you are doesn't happen overnight. You have to take it one day at a time and one thing at a time. My mother, on August 5th 2018, flew for the first time at the age of sixty-two. It's never too late according to Ecclesiastes 3:1, "There is a time for everything, and a season for every activity under the heavens." I know not everyone believes in the word of God so below are a few quotes from other resources;

- "Be the change you wish to see in the world." Mahatma Gandhi

- "If there is no struggle, there is no progress." Frederick Douglass

- "Change your thoughts and you change your world." Norman Vincent Peale

- "Only I can change my life, no one else can do it for me." Carol Burnett

- "I can't change the direction of the wind, but I can adjust my sails to always reach my destination" Jimmy Dean

- "If you don't like something, change it. If you can't change it, change your attitude." Maya Angelou

Chapter 10: "I Smoke Two Joints"

Song by The Toyes 1996

Once I came out to my mom, I could care less who else knew. Some family members looked down on me and of course some tried "praying the gay away". Chile what they did not know was I had been trying to do that for years, crying on the floor praying to God to remove this thorn from my side. I did not want to kill myself, but thought of doing so quite often. That's what self-hate and depression will do to you. During my prayer time, I would ask God to take me from this earth, I wanted to be with Him, I wanted to be carefree, I wanted to be "normal". I'd be tossing and turning at night struggling with my sexuality and spirituality, all while thinking about how bad I wanted some guy's mouth on my manhood. I remained faithful to God and the church for as long as I could.

Now out of the closet and seeking spiritual guidance from my youth leader, I was informed by him I was no longer allowed to be alone with another male. There was already a rule that males could never be alone with females which meant I wasn't allowed to be alone with anyone at all. WHAT THE HELL? So now you're taking away my freedom? Rather than fight it I submitted to this new directive. I did my best to cope. I relocated where I sat at church from the middle center behind the sound booth to the front side of the congregation. This was where the majority of the pastors and their families sat, along with the prayer warriors (one of which I use to be). If you are not familiar with how some churches are set up some of them have people sitting in the back called prayer warriors. Their job was to be silently praying throughout the entire service for souls to be saved. It was there in that new location of the church where I met this girl named Sam. She was a hoot and I knew we would be life-long friends. We would write notes and pass them back and forth to each other during church service. Back then there was no texting back and forth so we'd pass hand written notes. Just thinking about it makes me feel old because it seems like so long ago. (Side note: I actually started writing this book with pen and paper, old school baby!) Her dad was a pastor, well respected and an all-around put together guy. He was tall, dark and handsome with great teeth and had a beautiful wife and kids.

The note passing was our thing and would take place during most of the sermons. Sam and I had missed a lot of the sermon doing this, but it's how we got to know each other. One Sunday morning a shift happened, the notes went from funny, silly and church related material to the sharing and inquiring of more personal information. I was so tired of smiling in the faces of these church folks, knowing they were talking about me behind my back. I had figured that I would give them something to talk about, a sort of *run and tell that*! Pondering the thought for a moment, I decided to follow through with action. On that little piece of paper that had been written on and folded up several times, I wrote *I'm gay!* I folded it yet again then handed it to Sam. My hands were sweating, throat damn near closed up, and had little tears welling up in my eyes. I was both nervous and scared. She read it, wrote something down then passed it back to me. Was I ready for this? Was she going to openly rebuke me? Tell her parents? My mind was racing a mile a minute. I opened the note and was surprised when I read the two words she had written. Those two words changed my life and I believe the way I would approach things from then on out. The words were *Me too!* I was in shock, and could not believe my eyes. The hardest part of coming out, like I said earlier, is the reaction of those you are coming out to.

Thank God the people closest to me, accepted it as well as they did. Hell, my sister said she had figured it out about me since I was little. I was happy for Sam to trust me with her truth as I trusted her with mine. Now, I was looking around that church thinking, *So, this is where all the gay people are.* When Sam's family found out about her sexuality she was forced out of their home and on to the couch at our home. My mom and dad agreed to take her in. Do you know how many LGBTQ people are kicked out of their family's home when they come out or are found out? Trust me, thousands if not millions around the world. That's what I loved about my family. Though my dad did not say much about me being gay, I knew he loved me regardless. We already had a house full, but that never stopped my parents from taking a friend in that needed a place to lay their head. We had taken in several of my friends throughout my time living with my parents. I was blessed to never be that kid wondering where my next meal would come from or where would I sleep at night.

Excited that Sam was now there all the time with me, we became even closer. Actually, we became extremely connected and I mean to the point of us deciding to leave the church. Eventually Sam had found a place and was preparing to be on her own. I was excited for her and a bit jealous. Just off from the campus of Southern University was a little older apartment building with a small unit with her name on it. I'd visit frequently and spent many nights at her place. We would spend our time listening to Bob Marley and smoking weed. We would smoke like there was no tomorrow. I can't believe some of the crazy things we did. For example, we'd lace our blunts with other drugs and get very high. Hell, I didn't even know what lacing meant back then but we did it. One night I was leaving the club with friends and was the one in the driver's seat with a car full of gays, puffing and passing. While stopped at a red light, with a little crack in the window to let some of the smoke out, a police officer jumped on the hood of the car just as the light turned green. He was holding on for dear life and instructed me to follow a guy they had been chasing on foot. When I tell you I almost shitted myself in fear, I am not lying. I was trying to drive normal while also trying to get the others to throw the blunt out of the window because I did not want the officer to smell the weed. I knew he'd immediately make me pull over and arrest all of our asses. It was too much going on and I thought for sure I would be in jail that night – BUT GOD! As we gained a closer distance to the guy on foot, the officer slid off the car and thanked me with a tap on the hood. That was drama we had not anticipated.

Nightlife was fun for me and my friends. We would go to all of the gay clubs in the city. One night we met a lesbian couple and we all became a click. When you saw me; you saw them. Hanging with these three girls really opened my eyes and I knew without a doubt, God was real. Our sleepovers consisted of a wake up and light up. Passing the blunt all day until we couldn't do anything but think of food. Another night with me behind the wheel, I remember Sam asking "Tim, are you driving on the right side of the road?" My reply was "Girl, I don't know, if I see headlights I will just change lanes". What was I doing with my life? I had an eye-opening experience that night, everyone needs that eye-opening experience. More often than once you need to say to yourself, *I don't want to be this or that.*

Chapter 11: "Window Seat"

Song by Erykah Badu 2010

I still had a desire to experience new things and see the world. One day I got dressed, jumped into my small two door deep blue, used 1990s Geo Metro and drove over to the mall with my driver's license and high school diploma in hand. I walked into the U.S. Army Recruiting Office and made a short announcement, *I am ready!* They knew I was interested in enlisting since high school. I would always go out of my way and stop by to speak to the recruiters every time I was in the mall. Every time I did they'd try to enlist me on the spot but I would always inform them that when I am ready, you will know! Well the time had come and it was now, my mind was made up and I was ready. My paperwork was processed but I had to come clean about my use of marijuana. Shortly after that sit down with my recruiter, it was time to make things official. The drive was a long one. New Orleans was where we had to go to MEPS, which is the Military Entrance Processing Station. Only an hour away from Baton Rouge, but the journey had to take us about two hours. Why you ask? Because the other three guys in the car with me were also marijuana users and we all were forced to drink a gallon of water while on the way to MEPS. The drinking of water cleaned our systems so the marijuana's THC level wouldn't show in our drug test, boy I tell you them recruiters did what they had to do. Clearly, we all had different peeing schedules and they had to pull over numerous of times for us to relieve ourselves. Some of those times were on the side of the highway and we would just step out and piss on the shoulder.

We arrived to the station and did all of our processing, paperwork, physical evaluation and then the swearing in. OH MY GOD, when I got in that room full of future soldiers and they told us to raise our right hand to take the oath and be sworn into the military, reality hit and hit hard. I was nervous but ready. After being sworn in as enlistees, we were assigned dates and locations for our basic training. Ft. Know, Kentucky was where they sent me, right in the cold winter month of January. It was an all-male training facility and I heard it was one of the more difficult boot camps. I was so ready to get the hell out of Louisiana that going there didn't faze me one bit. I was ready to travel the world and see things I had never seen and experience things I had never done. Unfortunately, my mom did not have the same enthusiastic mutual feelings or visions for me in the military as a full-time soldier. She wanted me home close to her and preferred that I'd rather participate in the Army Reserves. She won that battle because I love my mom with all of my heart and didn't want to disappoint her. After a long conversation and research, I decided to enroll as a reservist mainly because I could always, in the future, reenlist as active duty. That winter of 2000, shortly before I was to leave to go to basic training, I stood in the bathroom with a pair of scissors in hand. The dreads I had been growing for two and a half years were now down to my shoulders, but now I had to cut them off. I do not recall how long I stood there in the mirror trying to build up the courage to do it. I had no idea that it would be this emotional either, besides it was just hair. In a matter of seconds, my dad quietly entered the bathroom, took the scissors out of my hand and in one swift move grabbed three of my dreads right above my forehead and cut them off. There was no turning back from there, we continued cutting until they were all gone. A week or so later this 19-year-old was off to basic training for the United States Army.

It was my first time flying and I did not miss a beat to make sure I got on that plane. Upon arrival to our destination airport, we were bused over to the base. Let me tell you that first day was terrifying. If I can remember correctly the windows on the bus were dark so we could not see out of them. The drill instructors, DI's, drill sergeants, or drills were a few of the names we had for them. They jumped on the bus and began screaming in our faces and telling us to get off and into formation. Once outside shit got real for us all. We were forced to repeatedly pick up and put down our heavy duffle bags which held all of our belongings, so you know it was heavy. We ran here, ran there, did push-ups, jumping jacks, and whatever else they told us. Spit was hitting our faces like rain drops as the drill instructors yelled at us right up in our faces. They were so close that if they stuck out their tongues it would touch your face. It was one of the longest days I had ever experienced in my life. If you have ever seen the movie GI Jane, it was similar. Boot camp is tough no matter what branch of the military you enlist in. They cursed us up and down, left and right, called us outside of our names and made fun of our physical appearances. They were just RUDE; rude I tell you! But it was and is their job and the first week, hell week, is meant to be the hardest. At the end of that first day you were given a decision to leave if you felt you could not continue on. I believe two guys raised their hands and were sent back home. I will admit that I had questioned why I didn't raise my hand and get the hell out of there. But I wanted this, my dad did it, so could I. As the week went on the two minutes in the restroom, the 'chew now taste later', waking up early and the running until you threw up all got a bit easier to handle. I could go on and on, but l am sure you get the point. It was freezing cold there. I had never seen so much snow in my life. I had actually only seen snow maybe twice in my life, but nothing on that scale. It was harder to adjust to my new normal mainly because of the cold weather. I was from the deep south and more accustomed to mild winters and hot summers. In spite of it, I adjusted and made it through. Every morning you could hear the horns over the speakers that were throughout the base. Reveille is a bugle or trumpet call signaling the start of the day. The name comes from the French word reveille, which means wake-up. I can still hear the cadences from the troops running by coming through the window.

> *"One mile – No sweat*
>
> *Two mile – Better yet*
>
> *Three miles – Gotta run*
>
> *Four miles – Just for fun"*

This conversion from civilian to soldier was a great journey because the military changed the way we walked, talked, dressed and thought. Till this day I still say, "Stay alert, stay alive, stay ready so you don't have to get ready; and Hydrate, hydrate, hydrate!" Nine weeks of learning how to shoot assault weapons, conduct hand to hand combat, perform road marches, sleep in the fields, and make beds were all worth it. The time was approaching to become a soldier. The last requirement was a twelve-mile rucksack road march. Our rucksacks housed everything we would need to survive in the field. The rucksacks weighed around 75-95 pounds and we carried them on our backs. We wore a bullet proof vest, a helmet and had weapons in hand, typically a military assault rifle. Prior to our twelve-mile march, we first had to complete the three, six, and eight-mile marks. This was a process that we were properly trained and prepared to get through. After hours of marching each of us was sweating bricks of perspiration although the outside temperature was in the teens; but it felt more like single digit temperatures. Finishing that march was a huge deal and there was a ceremony that took place right after the completion of it. At this ceremony we were called soldiers for the very first time, a feeling any solider will never forget.

The morning after was the warrior's breakfast that featured all you can eat of every breakfast food imaginable. Graduation was that evening and it was a bitter sweet day for me due to the fact that not one single family member would be in attendance. Yes, I was heartbroken, but I joined alone and went through training alone, so hell at that point I was like *fuck it!* My mom had never flown and the drive was too long and expensive. I understood but was ready to cut the umbilical cord that kept me attached to family. My mom not being there really upset me deep down inside because it was one of my biggest accomplishments in life. Thankfully my Dalton, Georgia battle buddy and his family were there for me and allowed me to tag along for their family outing. After the graduation we were able to have a few hours off base with family. On that day my family were some country southern white folks from Dalton, Georgia whom I had met for the first time – YEE HAW!

Ft. Jackson, South Carolina was where I landed next for AIT, which stands for Advanced Individual Training. It is basically job training for the MOS (Military Occupational Specialty) you choose. I went in as a 71L, an administrative assistant. The job had an interesting approach to training us because after just a few weeks, I spent most of my days in class in front of a computer screen typing or playing word games. You see, these games were a part of the curriculum, I was not just goofing off. We still had early morning wake up and exercise sessions which wasn't too bad and not as difficult as basic training. Basic training is brutal on the mind and body. This was more refreshing and laid back. After classes were completed we actually had free time to do as we pleased like go shopping and hang out at the PX (Post Exchange), which was like the Military Walmart. The PX had everything you wanted and you always spent more money than intended.

Upon returning home with my certified 71L paperwork in hand, I was ready to go to my unit and check in. Once I did, I was settled in and ready to begin the one weekend a month drills I had to participate in. Our workload wasn't too bad, we did some training here and there and a little bit of work. There was a gym in the back that we would utilize frequently. Then we had our annual two-week training which we called AT (Annual Training). We normally would go to some military base in the middle of nowhere for those two weeks of training. It was more hands-on training like participating in the shooting range for target practice, team building exercises and things of that nature. They would house us in barracks or they would have lodging, which was basically a hotel. I am grateful for the training I'd received because it taught me some really positive things about working with others as one unit.

Chapter 12: "1-2-3"

Song by Gloria Estefan 1988

During the years when people made more use of pagers and beepers, 143 were three numbers that was sent and received often. Are you familiar with this number? It is slang for *I love you* and simply represents the number of letters in each word of the phrase. Those three words are so meaningful and priceless. When was the last time you said to someone I love you? Love hit me hard when I fell head over heels in love with this particular man. He was a part of my life and I wasn't ashamed of letting him know how much I loved him. For the sake of this book we'll call him Howard and to be honest I cannot recall how we met or when exactly we were together. I do know that I loved that boy, and he loved me. I am quite sure we more than likely met at a club or through a mutual friend. Regardless of how it happened, I do know we hit it off fast. Howard and I did everything together, we even started working at Blue Cross Blue Shield together. It was early fall of 2000 and my full-time job was as a data entry clerk at Blue Cross Blue Shield via the Manpower temporary work agency. I loved that agency, and was drawn to them because my sister had used their services before. They kept me employed there for about two years.

After just a few months, Howard was living with me in my room under my parents' roof. I could not believe this was actually happening, but it was. We only wanted to stay there a few months to save our money and move into a town-home we had our eyes on closer to our job. Between the two of us, I was the one with a car so we needed to be closer to work just in case something was to happen to the car. I will never forget the day we were packing up the car to move. As my dad was helping us load all of our belongings into the trunk, he paused, looked me in the eyes and asked "Are you sure you want to do this?" My dad was never the one to show much affection so this kind of caught me off guard and had me wondering where he was going with this question. My reply was "Yes dad I am sure." His comeback to me was "I love you". If my memory serves me correctly this was the first time, I as a grown man, heard my dad say those three words to me. I had just heard spoken out loud, that 143 beeper message or an I love you from my dad. There was a slight pause and he continued "I just want you to be happy." That moment meant the world to me, and still makes my heart smile when I think about it. My dad was NEVER going to talk to me about being gay so that was his way of saying he was okay with it. Howard and I moved into that two-bedroom town-home.

We were so excited to now have our own space. On the first floor was the living area, kitchen, a half-bath and dining room; on the second level were the bedrooms and a second bath. Our unit was the last one on a dead-end street, which we loved because we did not have to deal with any traffic. We were within walking distance to a CVS, a few gas stations and the "devil" as I called it which was a predatory payday loan office. When I tell you that we were robbing Paul to pay Peter, believe me when I say that we were barely getting by. It was my first time on my own as an adult and it was not easy. I was maybe 21-years-old and I believe he was slightly younger. Those payday loans were how we got cash to pay bills. We both had a loan and they were due for payment on different dates, so it worked out that when he would pay his I would renew mine, and when I paid mine he would renew his. This cycle was a hard thing to break. We were penny pinching and it was not fun at all. When something was wrong with the car, we had to walk to work because we didn't have any money to fix it. It was a nice long hike too but we made it happen. One day, a coworker saw us walking, picked us up and told us to just let her know when we needed a ride. I thought that was very kind of her.

I loved Howard but he came with some issues. For one, he was an habitual liar and he would lie through his fake ass teeth in a heartbeat, oh sorry, his real teeth *rolls eyes*. We fought a lot too. One night I found a bag of porn DVDs and magazines he had hidden from me. I wondered, why did he have to hide these? Hell, we could have enjoyed them together. That right there raised my suspicion about him and I began to worry that there may have been more that he may have been hiding from me. That day when he walked through the front door I was waiting for his ass. I was sitting on the stairs waiting like an old mean father ready to scold his teenage daughter who came home after curfew. The bag with his porn stash was in the middle of the floor and I began questioning him about it. I always knew when he was lying and like clockwork he began doing

73

it. I swear to God I blacked out and the next thing you know I had him by the throat with one hand, as his feet were dangled a few inches from the ground. I finally let him go once he looked like he was about to pass out. He was so upset, which he had all right to be. He ended up walking out and headed over to my mom's house on foot which I knew took him a good couple of hours. He was that angry and determined to get away from me. He stayed with her for a few days. We eventually made up and he came back home. Unfortunately, our relationship didn't last that long, I believe we were together a little over two years. The relationship had run its course. I moved back in with my parents once the lease on the town-home expired. I don't regret being with him because it taught me a lot about trust and love.

Chapter 13: "911"

Song by: Wyclef Jean Featuring Mary J. Blige 2010

On September 11th, 2001, I was at work for drill at the reserve unit. My unit was literally a mile or so from where we lived, so I would often walk there. I was outside having a smoke break that beautiful morning, then all of a sudden, someone came up to me and announced that everyone was required to report to the conference room immediately. It sounded urgent, so I put my cigarette out and hauled ass to the conference room. Like most people, I will never forget that dreadful day. As we filed in one by one, we saw the images on the big screen television that was on and positioned ourselves in the front of the room to watch what was happening. It was a horrific visual of one of the twin towers in New York City on fire. There were large billows of smoke rolling out of the side of the building. Our eyes were fixated on the screen when all of a sudden, we saw something slam into the second tower. Was that a damn plane that just struck the building? When that happened, I recall looking with fear in my eyes across the table at my friend and fellow soldier. She began fidgeting with the hair at the back of her head. Before I could say a word, she pulled out her fake weave bun and threw it on the table and said "This going to be a long ass day!", and it was.

We were on lock down until the next day. We had to call and inform family members that we would not be home for a while, it was a very scary day. I remember seeing my mom come to pick up her car from the unit. I at least tried to wave to her as they checked the car for explosive devices under and around it with mirrors. Not long after, I mean it had to be days later, I was called into the unit. It was news I kind of expected, the orders were in and we were being deployed. My duty was to go down a roaster and inform all the soldiers by phone of their deployment, the day they needed to report to the unit and what they needed to bring. Everyone was full of fear of the unknown, most of us were so young, not even 21-years-old yet. At the time, I was in a relationship with Sam. Our special song was *I Am Ready for Love* by India Irie.

I had met him in the summer of 2001 while I was out for a run around the neighborhood, shirtless and free balling. I swear every corner I got to, there at the stop sign or red light was him sitting in his car looking at me while sipping his 40-oz beer with the brown paper bag over it. Yeah, I like my men feminine in the bed and a bit more boyish outside, not thuggish just boyish. Well dressed, well spoken, groomed, street smart yet educated with book smarts. Any who, after a few blocks of this repeated encounter, I had to admit that he was kind of cute, so the next corner we locked eyes and I asked him "You like what you see?". He nodded indicating that he did, then motioned for me to come approach the car. I did, leaned onto the side of his car door and stuck my head into the lowered window of his old two door Cadillac. We chatted for a bit, before I jumped in the car and enjoyed a brief joy ride with him for a few blocks. Before dropping me home we exchanged numbers. We kept in touch and began dating shortly after. I loved that dude, 5'6", light skinned, thin like I like them. From his long hair that was braided most of the time and his not so perfect teeth, I loved it all. I had to let him go right before deploying though because I did not want him waiting for me or having to lose me while I was overseas in Kuwait. He gave me an India Irie CD and a teddy bear before I left, which was so sweat. I still have that damn teddy bear and my mom hates the name I gave it. Sammy is the bear's name. You may be thinking I named it after Sam which is partially true. You see my dad use to mess with a woman named Tammy while he was with my mother and Sammy popped in my head. I won't get deep into my dad's infidelity, but know it was just another example in my life that wasn't perfect. He was a great dad but not the best husband. Unlike my dad with Tammy, Sam was a love I will always remember and be reminded of through that teddy bear.

Chapter 14: "Hold My Mule"

Song by: Shirley Caesar 1997

The time for deployment had arrived and Fort Polk, Louisiana was where we went for the mobilization process. We were injected with all types of needles and received all of our necessary medical requirements before we could be deployed overseas. Sleeping in old World War II barracks filled with asbestos was no fun. I think they were trying to kill us before we headed out. I had all four of my wisdom teeth removed there in Ft. Polk and that amusingly did not stop me from having a good slice of pepperoni pizza days later. Pizza is my favorite food and my friends would just laugh as I used my front teeth to chew a slice like an old toothless man. A few weeks had passed, and it was time for families to come hang out on base for a few hours to say their goodbyes. The next day we were on our way to Kuwait. The flights there were long and felt endless. I mean it was twenty plus hours in an aircraft and I hated it. Everyone was a little nervous and afraid of the unknown. We were going to war and had no expectations other than staying alive.

We arrived in Kuwait safely. I ended up making that trip five more times. I liked being overseas. I was finally out of Louisiana and away from my mom which gave me a sense of independence and freedom as a young man. I extended my tour three times, with each tour lasting about six months. For two years Kuwait was home for me while I served for both Operation Iraqi Freedom and Operation Enduring Freedom, between the years 2002-2006. That place was deathly hot though! The temperatures would reach highs of 140 degrees and the sand storms literally felt like someone was throwing hands full of tiny pebbles at you with no mercy. Thankfully after the first few months we were no longer living in a warehouse and sleeping on cots. Those ugly green fold up cots where not comfortable at all, and they had to have at least a thousand or more soldiers in that damn warehouse.

We had to build makeshift walls with blankets or hold up cardboard barriers in front of each other just to get dressed and or change clothes. I mean seriously we would have to walk a half a mile in flip flops, on that hot ass sand to get to the showers and restrooms which were housed in those large POD storage containers. We later moved into almost a dorm room situation which was fine by me. The soldiers would share a common area that contained a restroom and a space to eat or lounge. Beyond that space were two rooms which each contained two sets of bunk beds. I worked at a desk inside one of the warehouses which thank God had air conditioning. There were some soldiers working and living in other areas of the base that were not so pleasant; tent city was the name of one of those living quarters and it looked just like it sounded. There were tents as far as the eye could see. It was a short ten – or fifteen-minute walk and I'd go and visit some of my friends who were housed there, attend a church service or meet someone for lunch. Did I say church? I sure did! Our base, Camp Arifjan, actually had the largest church service held. We eventually had to move services from the chapel which sat about, 75 to 80 people, to the theater which allowed a few hundred to attend. I was the master of ceremony every Sunday, you know, the MC, the hype man. I was also a part of the Praise Dance Ministry. Some may refer to this as liturgical dance, worship dance or prophetic dance. I also went through a course for Ministry training, before service those interested would meet up for pastoral training. We would dissect the bible verse by verse, pray and share about the major responsibilities of the ministry.

Even at my church back home, the megachurch, I had gone through a lot of training, retreats, and even a mission's trip to Mexico while still in high school. While in preparing for our missionary trip, us teens would walk the streets of downtown, entered local businesses and busy shopping centers collecting donations in return for a prayer to get us to Mexico. Going to Mexico gave me my first experience of traveling to another country and it was life changing. I recommend that if you have not had the experience of seeing how people live in a third world country, plan a trip to visit one because it will change your life. I'm not saying Mexico is third world, but there were parts of it that surely were. We cried and prayed nightly, it was such an eye opening and humbling experience.

As Americans, we were so blessed and did not even realize it until we saw the conditions others had to live in everyday of their lives. Something like clean running water was common for us, but not for them. Our normal was their luxury. Normal regular things like air conditioning in almost every home and business in the United States wasn't found in abundance in Mexico. Even the convenience of access to new clean clothes or shoes were some things we'd took for granted. While there, we gave away so much stuff to those in need. Our mission was to help them with their little clay church. The inside of it only had a few benches and some chairs. To help let any cool air circulate they had cut holes into the walls of the little hut to help with the air flow. We helped clean and paint that church, attended the service and praised God with them. Although we had no earthly idea what they were saying without the interpreter, there was a universal language that was present and visible to us all. What we saw were smiles, hugs, eyes full of excitement and hope, clapping, singing, dancing. It was such a beautiful thing to see. These young people, and I mean some as young as five years old, had little to nothing but had hearts full of joy and thanksgiving. They just wanted to praise God. At night we would have a gathering and discuss things we had learned that day, and all the things we were grateful for or took for granted.

Although I still had my struggles, the church was my bandage. I don't care who you are or what you say, we all need a bandage for everyday wounds received from this thing called life. It could be a friend you trust that you can to talk with, taking a trip, going to a musical, enjoying a concert or maybe even a reading a good book. Whatever outlet you feel would help just do it, mine was church. The joy of music, the fellowship, the release of tears, the lifting of burdens all happened for me in the church. I always felt so light and free after a good ole church service. And the church still has that effect on me today!

Here I was across on the other side of the world in another country, in the Middle East still seeking that comfort through the church. Why was this bandage still needed by me all the way in Kuwait? I know what some of you may be thinking. Here I was in the middle of a desert that was dry, meaning liquor was not available for purchase. No drugs were around. But you better believe they had cigarettes and homosexuals, and you bet your bottoms we had a few cruising spots to choose from. Cruising? Must I tell you everything? Ok, cruising in the gay community basically means a spot to meet, pick up and/or hook up with someone. Bath houses are well known spots for guys to meet up and have sex. Yes, I met, hooked up and had fun with several guys while overseas. In the bathroom stoles, port-a-potties or in the barracks, we did not give a shit, we did what we had to do to get off. Gays may not have been open in the military but we were up in there doing our thing, a lot of trade was getting down too. That last stall in the bathrooms you did not only find a toilet, but also a glory hole that you can tell some guy took his sweet time creating with a very sharp object. If the guy next to you tapped his foot, it meant he wanted to hook up. The floor was also made of a metal that reflected shadows so if the guy next to you was jacking off you would see it. We had wants and needs damn it!

Ironically, I actually met a lover at one of the spots. We would write notes on the bathroom stall's wall to each other. Finally, we started emailing. Oh yeah, we had created special emails for this purpose alone, then eventually agreed on a day and time to meet up face to face. We dated for a good year but then his unit relocated to Doha, which was about an hour away from Arifjan. Whenever I was there which wasn't often, we would meet up to see each other and at least have lunch together to catch up. He was a church boy as well, and was on the praise dance team in Doha, so when we had large events they would come dance and we would get to spend time together. State side and once back home I drove from Baton Rouge to Jacksonville, Florida to visit him. It was about an eleven-hour road trip. I had met his friends and mother. It was around Christmas time and we had a good time because we put up the tree and made some homemade pizza. He was another guy who after having sex with him, we would cry and pray together. Don't let the politicians fool you, there was a lot of gay sex going on in the military before it became legal.

Kuwait was an amazing experience and I had my share of fun when I could. Believe it or not there was a white girl I had started dating as well. On stage, she would pray in the pulpit right before I came up and during service she'd sit next to me with all the other ministers. I ended up breaking up with her though because she wanted to get a little too serious with me. I had let her know about the battle with my sexuality. She spoke of marriage and children and I could no longer lead her on because I didn't want those things with a woman. Even after telling her, she wanted to pray for me and still be with me. She was even willing to have sex with me to "fix" me. Heterosexuals don't get it, we don't need to be fixed because this is who God created us to be and having sex with the opposite sex surely will not do a thing to change us. This girl was in love, but when I tell you she was so innocent and pure, she really was that. She was a cute little soft spoken, Bible toting, tongue speaking, holy ghost filled woman and I had to stop that relationship. I was not going to pretend to be someone I wasn't. Today, she is happily married to a black man of God. The guy I was seeing is also happily married to a black man as well. Despite it all Kuwait owes me nothing, I had a great experience and met some amazing people. My church friends and I hung out frequently, we worked out together, ate together, chilled out in each other's office space and even visited churches around the base together. Sometimes, our fellowships went hard and long. We were always ready to have church, well at least I was. They hated "playing church" with me, because I would always start crying and praising God for real. It would start with them saying,"Thank Ya! You been so good to me...." on and on they would go, then I would start sobbing and shouting uncontrollably. "Ya'll just don't know...I could have been dead.". It always ended with, "See we can't never play church with him around!". Those were some good times.

Chapter 15: "I'm Still Here"

Song by Dorinda Clark 2002

I was grateful to be alive. It was the truth and I wasn't afraid to praise God and shed a tear for Him sparing my life not once, not twice, but multiple times. I love the line to a gospel song which says, "When I think of the goodness of Jesus and ALL He's done for me, my soul cries out Hallelujah!". It's a very popular saying in the church as well. That's how I felt and will until the day I die. Below are a few times I could have been killed but for the mercy of GOD! The enemy tried many times to take me out and end my life, but when you have a calling on your life no matter what that calling is, the devil will try it. John 10:10 says "The thief comes only to steal and kill and destroy...". Here are just a few of the things that I am so grateful for the mercy of God which spared my life:

- I had just gotten paid and decided late that evening to do some riding up and down the street. I was also kind of cruising and had cash on me, but had the cash hidden under the mat on the driver's side. Sometime cruising could end up with some guy wanting or asking for money in exchange for sexual favors and I knew this. I saw this guy, picked him up and he led me to a dead end where he begins to try to fight and rob me. Somehow, he managed to get under the mat to the money. How in the hell he knew that money was hidden there blew me away, could he smell it? I am thankful he took that money got out the car and fled, things could have been a lot worst.

- One night I picked a woman up to give her a ride. I have no clue what happened next, she just began speaking in a strange language and I felt an evil presence. I really felt she was trying to put a spell on me or some hex to control me. So, I began speaking in tongues as I pulled the car over. Her ass couldn't have gotten out of the car fast enough, she hauled ass! That experience was so scary and had my heart beating out of my chest. It also taught me the power of prayer, the gift of tongues and faith. Matthew 17:20 says "…if ye have faith as a grain of mustard seed, ye shall say unto this mountain, Remove hence to yonder place; and it shall remove; and nothing shall be impossible you." KJV

- When I lived in New Orleans for a short period of time while in the army, I had gotten so drunk while hanging out in the French Quarter. When I left I thought I was good to drive, but I wasn't. **DON'T DO THIS!!!** Drinking and driving kills people and if it doesn't kill you or another, it can still cost you everything. An accident will cost you money and possibly some jail time with your license being suspended. I was driving on the interstate or freeway as some call it, going around a curve I thought I could handle with ease. In my drunken state, my judgment was off and I hit the side of the railing. When I say hit I'm talking about messing up the entire right front side up to the point where it was totaled, no longer able to be driven. That was very scary and really shook me up.

- On another cruising night I picked up a guy who led me to an abandoned park. It was dark and there was no traffic in the area. As I parked the car in the middle of this park near the monkey bars, he actually tried taking the keys out of the ignition. OH, HELL NO! I grabbed the keys and got out of the car, he also got out and made his way around to me and we began to fight. At one point he had a hold on me from behind and had an ice pick held to my throat. I remember throwing the keys right before that moment, that's when he got mad and pulled out the ice pick. I will never forget the feeling of that sharp ass cold object being pressed up to the side of my neck. I didn't know what to do, I couldn't think. The only thought I had was if he pushes it in I'm dead, BUT GOD! Once again, the heavenly language known as speaking in tongues began to flow out of my mouth. When I tell you that he ran like he had seen a ghost and to be completely honest with you, I believe he may have seen an angel that had come to protect me. Luke 4:10 says, "He will command His angels concerning you to guard you carefully."

89

Sharing things like that is not easy and very difficult to relive. I hope and pray this touches, reaches, helps or stops someone from making some of the mistakes I have made. Some of these things almost took my life. I don't think I have shared any of these stories with anyone, EVER! I have always been very private with my sex life and I sure in hell wasn't about to share with others about me cruising. It was and still is a very common thing in the gay community, but I am not the type to share or brag about those types of things. If you want to learn more about cruising, there is a book I read and own that has a section talking about the topic, the book is titled *The Joy of Gay Sex* by Charles Silverstein, Felice Picano (the story behind this book comes a little later). I am grateful for God's mercy and protection. I am here to share these stories to warn you to use safety and precaution in whatever you do.

Chapter 16: "Break Free"

Song by Ariana Grande 2014

After serving in the army in Kuwait for two years, it was time to return back to the states or as we call it in all military branches, state-side. I wasn't finished with my military career though and immediately signed up for two years of active duty at my reserve unit. So, here I was in uniform for another two years, but this time at home in Baton Rouge. I did the last nine months in New Orleans, which was a blast. We lived on Algiers Naval Base and worked on the base of Belle Chase. My plan was to visit family and friends after those two years was up then return home to reenlist. I just knew in my heart that another tour overseas would be in my near future because I really enjoyed being in another country. Well that was my plan – but God! I may have had all the plans in the world but God had other intentions for my life. In Proverbs 3:5-6 it says, "Trust in the Lord with all thine heart; and lean not unto thine own understanding. In all thy ways acknowledge him, and he shall direct thy paths."

I did so much shopping while in Kuwait and began to unpack it all when I returned home. Shopping was like a second job for me over there and I loved it! Once I settled back into the comforts of home, I drove over to Houston, Texas which took about four hours from Baton Rouge. I wanted to spend a little time with my sister and her family.

I had a great time. Even to this day I enjoy spending time with my beautiful sister now that we have a great relationship and get along pretty well. Long gone are the days of us fighting one another. I always enjoy seeing her and spending time with her family. My next stop was Dallas, Texas which was only four hours away from Houston. I went there to see my best friend Eric and his, at the time, lover. We had been communicating mostly through email during the two years I was overseas, so you know I was elated to see his face again. I stayed for a good week or so, we ordered pizza, they took me around to sightsee and out on the town to Cedar Springs which was and still is the gay area of Dallas. I was falling in love with that city. Wow, Dallas was amazing, especially coming from a small town. The buildings, the nightlife, the food and gayborhood were lit…HEYYYY!!! One evening as we sat down for dinner, at this not too fancy restaurant in the heart of downtown Dallas, I looked at my watch which had the date on it and realized what day it was. As I stared into my best friend's eyes I said to him, "Today is my last official day in the military". I know they weren't ready for what would come out of my mouth next. "Eric, I am staying here", I said to their delight. The couple looked at each other, nodded and told me I could stay with them until I found a place and that they would help me find a job. I was excited and had to call my mom right then and there with the news. Her response was delightfully affirming. She said that she'd known that would happen and wanted to know when was I coming to get my things. I believe being deployed really helped my mom understand I needed to live my life and she would be okay if I moved away. YES, the cord was cut, I was FREE! So, Dallas it was for the next two years. I got a job then an apartment and for the next two years I had a ball. Eric and I had a blast going out, meeting people and even lived together a few times.

Do you remember one of the original social media sites called *MySpace*? It was around before Twitter and Facebook. Ok, I am old, so leave me alone, but *MySpace* was popping about a decade ago. One day I met this guy Paul on it. He was from Detroit and was about to move to Dallas around the same time I had moved into my first apartment there. When he got to Dallas I had already known about him being a pothead, but it really didn't bother me much. He was young and I had been through that stage in life as well. One evening, we had agreed to meet up at a popular night-club that I would often frequent. That night, we'd bonded instantly. We had a great time talking, laughing and dancing into the late-night hours. I had gone outside for some air and there was a lady standing outside of the club selling roses. I instantly decided to buy one for him. He blushed and looked around as though he wanted to make sure people nearby saw him with his rose, it was so adorable and cute to watch. We ended the night with a kiss and for the next few days would spend hours on the phone together. He was living with his cousin in Arlington which was a good half hour to forty-five-minute drive which I made about three times a week to see him. He eventually came to my place to visit and I swear a month had gone by and he was moved in. I helped him get a job and, no lie, he did whatever he had to do to get to work, I loved that about him.

I remember one thing I did with Paul when we first started dating was to have a question and answer session with him. We would each compose a list of questions we wanted to ask one another and would sit at the dining room table for about an hour to bond and get to know each other better. Soon these fun and excited sessions turned into emotional and frustrating work. We were also having trouble with our sex life and I decided to go out and buy us a few books on gay sex. He kept saying I was too big, so I wanted to try to help him to relax or learn how to take it. With me being a top and not knowing about being the receiver of a larger sized man, I had to turn to books to help us. We each had one book we would read and took notes from and then exchanged before we got together to discuss. It got better and when we were intimate it was great, although sometimes he would just make me stop in the middle of the act which would leave me heated. That frustration led me to fussing at him and making him feel like a failure in the relationship. Most nights we would just cuddle and make out to satisfy us both.

Paul and I both had a passion for hair. I had always played in my mom's and grandmother's hair as a young child for money. I saw how it made them feel good and happy so doing hair was always in the back of my head. We both had dreads at one point and would spend some nights doing each other's hair while watching a movie. I began to think more seriously about becoming a hair stylist so searching for a cosmetology school in Dallas was the next step to making it a reality. I was already working a full-time job and they had no night classes available at the schools I wanted to attend. We had stayed together for two years and the relationship ended when I caught him in a lie about smoking weed in my apartment, I was not about to have it. I think that is why I can't stand weed to this day. He ended up going to school, which I was glad to see him do.

I started a new job in Ft. Worth, Texas basically doing the same thing I was doing in Kuwait. I worked the 12 a.m. – 8 a.m. shift, and I loved it. I remember one night a good friend of mine called me at about 3:00 in the morning while I was hanging out. She and I went to high school together when she was a he, yes, she was a transgender woman. Her mom wanted her to get out of Baton Rouge and move to a bigger and more open-minded city. Her safety was her mother's biggest concern. I looked at my phone wondering why the hell would Dee be calling me at this hour. I answered thinking it was something serious and wanted to know what was up. She asked if I could talk because she needed some advice. I walked out to the smoking area of the venue I was at and she began asking me how I could just pack up my things and move to a new city. She was considering moving to Atlanta. I told her to just move, take some clothes and pack whatever you can, just MOVE. I had let her know to only take what she needed and to sell everything else, throw it out, or give it away because she could replace all of it once she'd relocated. I reminded her that she was young, single and nothing was there to tie her down. My final word to her was to just do it. She did it and till this day she is still in Atlanta and is doing very well on her job. Though we don't see each other as much as I would like, I am glad to know I was a part of the reason she is in Atlanta and living her best life. Sometimes you have to take off the restrictions, discard the fear and just go for it!

Chapter 17: "The Circle of Life"

Song from The Lion King by Elton John 1994

I had been on my job as a contractor for about a year hoping to make it a permanent position when I and my coworkers got word that we were being laid off. We knew how business worked and figured an overseas move would be cheaper labor for the them. Jesus, this was the last thing I needed because I was already living with my best friend trying to make ends meet and get back on my feet. I was behind on my car note and on top of that my grandmother wasn't doing well back home. I am a firm believer that everything happens for a reason. Ecclesiastes 3:15 talks about this. I love the book of Ecclesiastes because it is full of wisdom. In there I found some verses in the beginning of the third chapter that resonated with me. The verses pretty much say that *Everything that happens in this world happens at the time God chooses; He sets the time for birth and the time for death, the time for planting and the time pulling up; and that there is a time for killing and the time for healing, the time for tearing down and the time for building.*

My mother called not long after my layoff to inform me that my grandmother, her mom, wasn't doing well and a visit from me was long overdue and that I should come see her. I got my Greyhound bus ticket, packed up some clothes and was on my way home. It was during one of the bus's stops to pick up and let off passengers that I got a call from my mom letting me know that my grandmother, whom we called MoMo, had passed away. With tears in my eyes, I got back on to the bus and to my surprise I saw a family member had boarded that was also Louisiana bound. Look at God! I was able to grab the seat next to her and she was there to comfort me in that moment, God has always been there on time for me. When I got home my mom and I drove to Opelousas to help her sister, my aunt and Godmother, with the funeral arrangements. We were running here and there like chickens with their heads cut off. We were off to the church, to the burial grounds, to the dry cleaners and then finally to the jewelry department of the women's store to choose some accessories for grandma. We wanted her to look beautiful in her casket. It is never easy losing a loved one and losing her was hard but we made it through. After she was laid to rest, life began to return back to our normal routines again. I had decided to stay with my mom for a while since I had the time now that I was without a job. A few months had passed by and I was still looking for work. One evening I received a phone call from my best friend Eric and he'd asked if I had come back to Dallas to pick up my car. I hadn't and a minute or so later after thinking about where I parked the car, it hit me, *damn they got me.* My car, my beautiful brand new 2000 something white Hyundai Tiburon, had been repossessed! Not having a steady paycheck made it hard to catch up with the payments. I was upset but there was nothing much I could do about it.

Putting the loss of my car behind me, one day the insurance woman stopped by to collect a payment from my mother for her policy. The lady would always come inside, sit and talk with her which sometimes felt like hours. Somehow, they got on the topic of hair and I was called into the room for her to inform me about this fairly new Paul Mitchell school that had just recently opened up in Baton Rouge. It was actually a Paul Mitchell partner school called Vanguard School of Cosmetology. Paul Mitchell is one of the best and well-known hair schools in the nation. I was too excited and decided to not look for work any longer and apply to cosmetology school. Because of the school's popular demand I was placed on a waiting list. I knew that my destiny would be in doing hair so I didn't mind being on the waiting list.

One August night, while I was in the computer room, my mom came in crying saying that she thought my dad was dead. She was about to lose her shit and was very hysterical. I tried to calm her down and asked her what happened and what was she talking about. She shared that she had gotten a call from someone saying he had been rushed to the hospital and was unresponsive when they'd picked him up. She told me to go check. He was at his other woman's house at the time of the incident so I knew exactly where to go. He had been fooling around with this chicken-head for some time now, and she didn't live too far away. I pulled up in my dad's old beat-up pick-up truck, in front of her little run-down house which looked and appeared to be a trap house, only to be handed his pants and wallet and told what hospital he was taken to. I took a peek inside of his wallet just to see what was in it because dad would always keep a little cash on him; and just as I had suspected this nappy head, cracked out looking bitch had taken all of the cash from out of his wallet. I was pissed and wanted to fight, but had to get to the hospital and did not need to be going to jail that night of all nights.

That night was scary, one by one family and close friends began arriving to Baton Rouge General Hospital as we all waited silently in that little panic room. If you ever had to wait in this room you know the feeling. While walking into the room, everyone is looking at you like you are walking the green mile. The green mile is a term referring to the death row at the Louisiana State Penitentiary. There, the prisoners who are to be executed are held in a separate area of the prison until it is time for their death. They then are made to walk on a green floor to the electric chair. There was a movie called *The Green Mile* showing this exact thing happening. At the hospital, while waiting on news about my father, the uncertainty was all so overwhelming as there was a chill in the air and fear on the faces. Thankfully, my brother's wife had a cousin that worked at the hospital which was a little more comforting than some random nurse delivering the news we all had dreaded to hear. My father's life was over as a result of a massive heart attack. Then the tears began to flow from all of us. It was one of the hardest things I have had to deal with to this day.

That night Stacy, my ex fiancé, was there for me which I am still grateful for today. While I was outside waiting on her a stranger, this black middle-aged woman, came up to me and asked what was wrong and whether or not she

100

could pray for me. I told her that I had just lost my father, and yes, prayer would definitely be ok. For me, prayer was always welcomed. As I had shared, I was born and raised in the church so without a doubt I wanted and needed that prayer. Also, like I'd mentioned earlier, everything happens for a reason. If I had not lost my apartment, job and car in Dallas, I would not have had the freedom to just stay and be present to be a support system for my mom. Just a few months after having to lay her mother to rest, now she had to deal with the death of her husband, it was a very difficult time for her. They had been married for almost 30-years so this was really hard for her. When they got married my mom was pregnant with me so that goes to show you that they had been together for some decades. He had been the love of her life. We had to do the same for dad as we did for Momo – pick out his clothes, get the church, find a casket, call the insurance companies.

The days leading up to his funeral were long, draining and seemed never ending. Throughout the course of the days prior to the funeral, we'd constantly received phone calls, cards, food and knocks on the door from visitors. Everything was just beautiful by the time we pulled it all together. The flowers were pretty, my dad looked so handsome and the choir was amazing. From the time the doors of the church were opened to the portion of the service dedicated to the saving of one's soul, we had church! When the preacher did the altar call, we took it to a whole other level and just about tore that church apart with praise, shouting and dancing. That chicken head, my dad's side chick, was in the back of the church the entire time, and was the only one to respond to the altar call. As she stood in front of the church crying, right in front of my dad's coffin, my mom stormed off to the side room behind the pulpit. My brother, sister and I of course ran after her to calm her down and let her know this was not about her, but it was a celebration for dad. I know just seeing her there was a reminder to my mother of my father's infidelity. It was a hard thing we as a family had to deal with right there at the funeral but we did not end up fighting and tearing the church up. Thank God my brother did not kill the mistress. I did tell her daughter that her and her mom were not welcomed on the burial site and if we saw them there we would kick their asses. Suffice it to say they did not show up!

During my dad's repass, my phone rang and I had Eric to answer because I couldn't re-live telling one more person that my dad had passed, especially right after leaving the burial grounds. To my delight it was the cosmetology school informing me of my start date. God will always shine a little light in the midst of the darkness. The first year of not having my dad around was very rough and took me some time to adjust to not seeing or hearing him. We still had all of the memories in the house like his clothes which we had to go through and get rid of. To our surprise though, while planning the funeral and getting all of the insurance policies together, we discovered dad had more than the two we had thought. Which meant that there was more money for mom. She was able to get a new car and pass down to me the 1996 Black Toyota Corolla my sister had given to her. Things were looking brighter and I started cosmetology school and finished in ten months. I was a member of several groups and became the manager of the advanced team of stylists. I loved every minute of cosmetology school. I was that student that always arrived early and left late; I was typically the last one to leave out on most days. The teachers in our school not only taught us how to do hair, but also taught us on being business minded, a better and more positive person and forced us to change our way of thinking. They even taught us how to improve our vocabulary in a more professional manner. Good interaction with the public and your clients is just as important as knowing how to do hair. Amongst the kits issued to us, which included several different combs, round brushes, blow dryers and what nots was also a book by Winn Claybaugh titled *Be Nice (Or Else)*. It's a really good read not only for hairstylist. I encourage you to check it out, you'll thank me later. Just when everything looked dark and out of control in my life, God showed up and blessed me. Won't He do it!

Chapter 18: "Never Give Up"

Song by Yolanda Adams 2001

Moving to Atlanta for a job was my next venture in life. While still actively enrolled in cosmetology school, I had a client that would book appointments with me to have her tight kinky locks shampooed, conditioned, blown out and styled with the fantastic Paul Mitchell products. The results of my work blew her mind. That led to her contacting her cousin and informing her about the quality of my craftmanship. The cousin's curiosity led to her searching and finding me on Facebook so that she could look through some photos of my work I had shared. She owned a salon in Jonesboro, Georgia which is a small town about twenty minutes south of Atlanta and not far from the region of the airport. She fell in love with what she saw although I was still working as a student in the school. She was so impressed that she offered me a job in her salon contingent upon my interview.

A good friend of mine from back home was living in Atlanta; so I reached out to him and arranged a visit to stay with him and his at the time lover. They welcomed me into their home with open arms, and showed me around the city and the gayborhood. It was like Dallas all over again. The visit was to meet with the salon owners, check their place out and interview for a stylist position. All went really well. I was hired and asked to come back during the busy season before school was to resume. Although I had not initially passed the state board written exam, which meant I did not have a license, they were okay with me still working for them. It seemed like every time I took that damn exam, you would have thought I was trying to become a doctor. I kept getting the exam with all the skin disease and foot funguses. Yes, we had to learn about all those things while learning about styling hair, our tools and products. I was fortunate that one of the salon owners, Tiffany, was from Baton Rouge as well. She and I later took a trip back home so that I could retake and conquer the exam. Eventually everything began to fall into place for me. I passed the exam and received my cosmetology license and was working behind the chair as a licensed professional. I had moved into a cute apartment not far from the salon and all seemed to be going right for me.

Unfortunately, a few months later the salon had to close its doors, I had gotten there too late to even build up a client base. They were trying to get a stylist there who would be consistent, reliable and help grow the business. To attract new clients, we use to have Zumba classes next door, teeth whitening and a foot detox system service. She really taught me a lot and opened my eyes to the hustle mentality here in Atlanta. I believe that all things happen for a reason and I refused to stress out about the situation. As much as I tried to stay calm, the panic, worry, and fear of the unknown creeped in! Then came the questions flooding my mind; *What about rent? Gas? What will I eat? Do I wanna find another job in this area?* I really didn't have much in my apartment. I had a futon in the living room, an ottoman, a laptop to watch movies on and a blow-up mattress in the bedroom. Every morning I would wake up on the floor due to a small hole in that mattress. One morning after waking up, I began to pray because I was fed up with living like this. I was disappointed in myself and felt like a loser. I would have to walk to many places in order to preserve on gas. To eat, I'd walk a mile to the Wendy's just to buy a burger and fries off of the dollar menu; and if I was down to having barely any money in my pocket, I'd get some ramen noodles from the gas station. At the time, I was attending a Full Gospel Baptist Church that was led by a well-known pastor from New Orleans, Louisiana. He'd opened up an Atlanta church after the Katrina hurricane devastated New Orleans and his church building. I began to cry and ask God for help and guidance. I could hear a still small voice saying *ask and you shall receive*. Matthew 7:7 confirmed what I had heard because it says "Ask, and it shall be given to you; seek and you will find; knock, and it will be opened to you." Sometimes God will answer your prayer or speak to you through the Word of God, I mean just reread that, It's HIS words…HELLO!!!!

My fingers began composing a private instant message on Facebook to several close friends and family members. The message went something like this…

"I just moved to Atlanta to pursue my career as a hairstylist and the first salon I began working at had to close its doors recently. I need money to pay rent and eat. If each of you can send at least $5, I can make it another month. Thanks in advance."

107

Three weeks later, rent was paid. I was so grateful and was walking around my apartment in tears worshiping and praising God. I was overwhelmed with the responses I began receiving in my inbox from loved ones, friends and military buddies. Below are just a few I can remember:

Check your mail, I just sent you a check.

I sent you two $100 gift cards and I DO NOT want you to spend this money on paying bills, treat yourself to some good food and go out on the town for a cocktail.

Remember doing my hair for free before a job interview I had? I got you, be on the lookout."

Just sent money via Western Union.

Go to MoneyGram in the morning, we have a little something, something waiting on you.

It was not only a humbling experience but it was also eye opening and showed me that obeying that still small voice will never disappoint. The scriptures say, "He replied, blessed rather are those who hear the word of God and obey it" Luke 11:28

I began applying for jobs at hair salons across metro Atlanta. One day, while online job searching, I came across one that I fell in love with because the website and photos of the space had caught my eye. I could see myself doing hair at this salon. I was tired of being broke and the person always asking and needing money, HELL NO, I didn't want to be that! I just wanted that money to get me by for ONE month because I am not the type of man to live dependent on donations. I needed to earn my own income and finding a job that was going to do that for me. The salon was a great space and was located in Chamblee, Georgia which was a good thirty to forty-five-minute commute from Jonesboro. That had me questioning whether to apply or not so I gave Tiffany a call for some advice. She encouraged me to just go for it because it was a great area and the people there were not penny pinchers like they had been in Jonesboro.

I cautiously went over my resume before emailing it and I believe I had my best friend take a second look at it as well. I was a bit nervous but determined. I had the resume attached to the email to the salon letting them know I wanted to apply for the position. My hands were sweating as my finger hovered over the keyboard key to send the resume. I said a quick prayer, closed my eyes and hit send. Just like that it was gone. I felt relieved after I sent it over and knew that all was in God's hands now. It was but a few days later that I was invited in for an interview. I found the place and took a seat up front, waiting for the young beautiful salon owner named Heather to come and conduct the anticipated interview. She was impressed with my presentation, well put together physical appearance and the photos of some of my work that I had in my look-book. I was offered the opportunity to do a live presentation and just a few days later I was there doing highlights and a haircut on a good friend of mine that accepted the role of my model as part of the stage two of the salon's interview process. Within a week I was offered the position and was working at the salon. All the stylists there were white women, I was the only black, only guy and only gay on staff. Talk about standing out like a sore thumb – that was me! It wasn't a problem but rather a good thing because people tend to be drawn towards uniqueness. I learned and grew a lot as a person and stylist at this cute, suburban hidden gem.

In less than two years, I went from working my way from the front desk, to styling behind the chair, to renting my chair and having my own small business in the salon. Wow, in those three years there I had accomplished a great deal and to me it was worthy of a pat on the back considering how broke I had been. Renting a chair or booth rental can be very rewarding and a great business if you have the discipline and clientele. Basically, you are your own boss with just having to pay to rent the chair. Unfortunately, Heather pushed me into renting before I was ready to handle it. I had been thinking about renting a chair, but knew I needed to wait at least another year or two. You need time to build up your clientele list in order to cover the cost for the chair rental each month. That first year of having a hair business to myself was the hardest as a stylist. Mind you, the salon was hidden so we didn't get walk-ins and my booth rent was twice the amount of my apartment. Being responsible for transportation, marketing, equipment maintenance and supplies was breaking me. I got behind on booth rent and she helped me for a while, then the shit hit the fan. One day Heather said "I am taking everything you make until you are up to date on your payments." It was tough hearing that, but as a business owner I understood why she had to make that decision.

Marta is Atlanta's public transit system and the train stop was not far from the salon. It was cheaper to take the train to and from work because it was only $2.50 one way.

Baby, let me tell you there were days I did not know how I would even get $5 to ride Marta. I had already gotten rid of my car at this point so I was totally dependent on public transportation. Because I was living in midtown I had no need for my car, I would walk everywhere. After moving there, I allowed myself a year of not using my car before I made the decision to get rid of it. I had to do something for extra money because my boss was not even allowing me to keep my cash tips. I needed a part time job to help ends meet. I was applying at Mac cosmetics, Sephora, and anywhere I thought I would enjoy working while making a little money. One day while pondering, I remembered seeing a salon that had recently opened two blocks from my apartment on the bottom level of one of the high-rises. I went online to search and find their number and gave them a call while on break at my job. I talked with the owner and inquired about a stylist position and due to them being fairly new, they were looking. YES!!!!

Heather fired Renee, the receptionist, after she saw her giving me print outs of my clients' information. Fearing I was going to leave and take them with me, the next day she told me not to return. Almost in tears, stomach in a knot, I began placing all of my belongings in a trash bag. I had no idea how I would get my entire station not only into that bag, but home on public transportation because it was big and heavy. I mean I had to take everything from my shears, blow dryer, and hair color to all of my hair clips. I could have gone and bought new ones but being that I was short on cash it wouldn't have made sense. Thankfully, a coworker felt sorry for me and took me back in their car to my little midtown studio apartment. Again, it all worked out because the salon in midtown was now going to be full-time instead of part-time. I began working at the new salon in the summer of 2014, and as of the time of this book's writing I was a full-time stylist there. Big windows surround the space where you can see everything happening in the salon, I love the open window concept. All of us stylists there are like family. I recall passing the salon right after it had opened, cuffing my hands to lean against the windows to take a look on the inside. It was so cute and was another salon I saw myself working in. It was like God was showing me what was in store for me. Follow your dreams, you never know what doors will open up for you.

Chapter 19: "Do You See What I See?"

Popular Cover Christmas Song

The title of this chapter is closer to the original book title I had in mind, so I wanted to share a bit on my thought process behind that phrase that was stuck in my head for about half way through my writing process. I would often ask myself and others *Are you looking?* or *Do you see?* There is a difference between the two. I have always been the guy to see things that others may not. People would show me a picture, let's say it is a group of family members on vacation and they are posed in the beautiful lobby of the hotel or the bed-in-breakfast they are staying in. I would be that person that would notice a painting in the background or some type of vase that would capture my attention. I would talk about that instead of the actual people in the picture. Although I obviously looked at the people, I saw other things, smaller things, the things and or details others would not even pay attention to. Even the meaning of the words *looking* and *seeing* are different. Looking means direction of one's gaze toward someone or something or in a specified direction. While seeing means perceive with the eyes; discern visually (spot, notice, detect) – be or become aware of something from observation or from a written or other visual source. You see the difference between looking and seeing now? One can look into the sky and the other can see a cloud, another could see that cloud shaped like a heart.

I, for some reason, always go back and think about the deeper message in the movie *Pretty Woman*, which is known as a modern update on the Cinderella story. If you have not seen it please check it out. The film stars Richard Gere and Julia Roberts and is a well-made movie. When I watch it, I always see the bigger picture. This wealthy guy picks up a woman who everyone else looked at as a prostitute because that was her profession; but he saw a beautiful and intelligent woman. He gave her an offer she could not turn down because he didn't see her as just some prostitute. He offered an upfront lump sum payment for her to stay with him for the weekend. They hit it off well and he learned more about her wit, charm and inner beauty. He looked beyond that street walker in her and saw her as a quality woman. Because of his ability to really see, it created a wonderful fairytale ending for the movie.

"Do you have eyes but fail to see, and ears but fail to hear?"
Mark 8:18

"Vision is the art of seeing what is invisible to others."
Jonathan Swift

"Every closed eye is not sleeping and every open eye is not seeing."
Bill Cosby

"Looking and seeing are two different things."
John Paul Caponigro

From this day forward, when you step out with friends, are at that table with the fancy white linen clothes waiting on your five-star experience, look around and see. See what people are talking about, see what you can take in, look around and challenge yourself; hell make it a game if you have to and see something you would normally not pay attention to. Maybe instead of looking at that waiter, the one that seems like she is ready to quit, worried that her world is crumbling down, has been on her feet all day and has had about all she can handle pause for a second. Instead, just maybe, you will see that older generous gentlemen slip her a great tip on the slide (meaning discreetly). Doing this is a game changer, I am a living witness. It helps you to begin looking on the brighter side of things in life. I mean no one would appreciate the sun as much without the clouds and rain storms every now and then. We would not be so happy to feel that nice cool breeze that welcomes us as we step into an air-conditioned building if it were not for the heat outside.

Try to live life with a grateful attitude and watch how things around you will begin to change. Have you ever tried affirmations? Affirmation is defined as the action or process of affirming something or being affirmed. Some of its synonyms are declaration, statement, assertion, proclamation, and pronouncement. If you have not tried affirmations I recommend finding a few that stand out to you, write them down and post them somewhere to see and recite them daily. Start off doing this once a week to give yourself some time to become accustomed to this. We are creatures of habit and it takes twenty-one days to create a new habit so once you are ready repeat daily at least twenty-one days consistently. Affirmations can be quoted all throughout the day. If you want to spend a few minutes on your break at work doing so, YouTube offers plenty of videos for your listening pleasure filled with great and powerful affirmations. Remember me talking about the book of James, the power of the tongue and the words that comes out of your mouth? Here are a few other quotes outside of the bible that speak of the power of words.

"Handle them carefully, for words have more power than atom bombs."
Pearl Strachan Hurd

"Words can inspire. And words can destroy. Choose yours well."
Robin Sharma

"Words have the power to destroy or heal. When words are both true and kind, they can change our world."
Buddha

"Your words are like orders placed with the universe, choose them carefully."
Law of Attraction Peal of Wisdom #6

"Begin to use the two most powerful words, I AM, to your advantage. How about, "I AM receiving every good thing. I AM happy. I AM abundant. I AM healthy. I AM love. I AM always on time. I AM eternal youth. I AM filled with energy every single day."
The Secret

If you have not read the book *The Secret*, you should. It speaks of the power of words and speaking things into existence. Affirmations, faith, and the law of attraction are all spoken about in the book and makes for a good read and a must for your home library. Now, don't you dare start looking at me and this chapter all crazy or sided eyed. I want you to rather see yourself getting into the habit of being a firm believer in affirmations. Yeah, you know I am talking to you, don't you roll your eyes at me! I want to see you become the best version of yourself in life so just do it!

Chapter 20: What's Your "That"?

Quote "It's better to hang out with people better than you because you'll drift in that direction." Unknown

Back in 2009, The singer Deborah Cox did a song called *Nobody's Supposed to Be Here* and she poses two questions in her lyrics which ask, *how did you get here?* and *do you want to be that?* I'm about to break some stuff down for you, so go ahead and grab a pen or pencil. Oh yeah baby, it is time to think, time to get real with yourself, time to question yourself and your surroundings. Be prepared for a shaking, a good cry, a shift, to be uncomfortable. You may even get a little mad or upset, if so...GREAT! Change does not happen until we reach that point of being fed up, that moment when your back is against the wall and the only way out is to move forward with your fist balled up in the fighting position and ready to swing at any negativity that comes your way. Changing is never easy, but it is possible.

"Don't be afraid to change. You may lose something good but you may gain something better"
Unknown

"Your life does not get better by chance. It gets better by change."
Jim Rohn

"Change the changeable, accept the unchangeable, and remove yourself from the unacceptable."
Denis Waitley

"For every positive change you make in your life. Something else also changes for the better – It creates a chain reaction."
Leon Brown

Have you ever experienced an off or bad day? You know, one of those days where you may feel like crap or nothing is going right. You may have a day where you are sick of **that** thing you can't seem to overcome. What is your **that**? Is it a friend or friend of a friend that never has anything positive to say? Is it that coworker who is always complaining? These are some examples of things I recognized around me that would have me saying *I don't want to be that*. Here's an exercise I want you to complete which asks you some probing questions about yourself and circumstances. Please complete them:

If I asked a close friend of yours about you, how would they describe you?

_____

_____

_____

_____

_____

_____

_____

Do you get upset easy and why? What is it that pushes your button?

_____

_____

_____

_____

_____

_____

_____

_____

What makes you have a bad day? Is it the weather? How about traffic? Is it something you can control? Do you wake up on the wrong side of the bed? (Just so you know I know it's a saying, but my bed is against the wall and only has one side to enter and exit). Think people, THINK!!! What gets under your skin? It may be this part of the book where I am acting like a 3-year-old asking you questions back to back before you can respond. Do you hate it? Are you getting upset? Tap, tap, tap I'm talking to you, Yes YOU! Am I hitting a nerve? If so GOOD, if not, even better! I just want to know what gets under your skin.

_____

_____

_____

_____

_____

_____

_____

_____

What type of vibe do you give off? Does that vibe attract or repel the people around you? And what does it attract and/or repel, what type of energy?

_____

_____

_____

_____

_____

_____

_____

I cannot and do not allow myself to be around negative energy because it is seriously like a bad taste in my mouth that I have to spit out before I move along. Most of my life I have been known as a happy person and the life of the party. I learned not to give in and fit in with my surroundings, but to influence or change the environment around me. So, if I walk into a room and everyone is gossiping, if they know me it will stop or they will acknowledge that I may not want to hear what they are talking about. If I don't know them I will try and change the subject or leave.

It's time for change, and change starts with one thing and person at a time.

The messy person...don't be that!
The gossiper...don't be that!
Negative all the time...don't be that!
Doubter...don't be that!

Scared...don't be that!
Stressed...don't be that!
Sad...Depressed...Broke...Lazy...Untraveled...
DON'T BE THAT!!

Keep your eyes open to those positive influences around you and allow them to mold and shape you into a better person. Not the other way around, if you have some negative, hateful, annoying and bitter folks around you... just RUNNNN!!! Turn away, do not look back. Oh, they are a close friend? Deal with it! Oh, it's your mother? Deal with it! I do not care who these people are, something different needs to happen. Whether it requires a good old fashion sit down study talk with yourself or another; or finally making a decision to cut them off completely. It may be difficult, uncomfortable and may even seem impossible, but trust and believe you can do it. Not long after making little changes that were spoken about throughout this book you will become that inspiration, that light, you will be that guy, that girl. You want to become the person that others will not just look at, but see. People will begin to tilt their head slightly to the side as they smile and say "I want to be that".

I wanted to end this book with a few words of praise from friends and family. I asked a few people to describe me in their own words, in short, as if they were telling another person about me. Below are the responses received and I was and am so humbled to have these people in my life and truly appreciate the kind words. Love ya'll!

"Timothy's positivity is contagious, he tells everyone he meets to live life without negativity. He is always a happy go lucky person, and will not allow anyone to steal his joy. He lives his life to the fullest every day without regret. His laughter is one thing people fall in love with when it is heard. He wakes up daily with love and happiness in his heart."
Deborah Keys, Mom

"Keys has the courage to LIVE for those of us that can only EXIST. And I mean that!" She also added "Your freedom for life is oxygen for my Facebook feed."
Military buddy

"Timothy's energy and smile are contagious! It definitely makes your day when you see him and his beautiful smile coming your way!"
Jason Atlanta

"We have been the best of friends since day one, and nothing has changed"
Love, Spiritual Mom

"Timothy has always taught me that one of the keys to life is positivity. I hope this book will inspire others as he inspires me to live and love life."
Latoya Griffin, Friend

"Your energy makes me smile."
DJ, Bartender

"Fun, loving, outgoing, meets no strangers and is always the life of the party."
Stephie Reni, Former Salon Owner/ Friend

"I've known Tim for about twenty years. That should tell you everything you need to know! To meet him is to have a friend for life!"
Khary Wilson, Long-time friend

My friend and neighbor told me there was a song that made her think of me "Way Back When" by Brenda Russell. "Way back when I saw magic, you can blame it all on your friends and your companions, I knew you way back when."
Lady Dee, Proud Friend

"Timothy Keys, I proudly claim you as my work husband. It has been almost 5 years and your positive mindset is nothing to be overlooked. And your incredible energy and happiness are contagious to everyone who crosses your path. You are not only an amazing friend and coworker, but have become a part of my family and have made a big mark in Kennedy's (her son) life. I am proud of you and look forward to watching your journey continue."
Stefanie H. Sanders

Made in the USA
Columbia, SC
10 June 2020